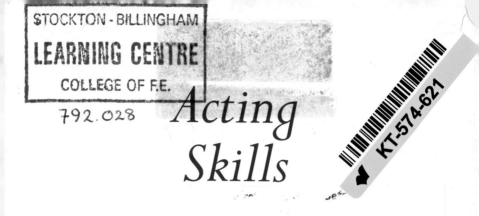

Acting
Skills

Acting Skills

2nd edition

Hugh Morrison

A & C Black • London

Second edition 1998
First published 1992
A & C Black (Publishers) Limited
35 Bedford Row, London WC1R 4JH

ISBN 0–7136–4932–1

A CIP catalogue record for this book is available from
the British Library.

The cover photograph is of *Marat*, taken by Chris Parker

Typeset in 10½ on 12 pt Photina
Printed and bound in Great Britain by
Biddles Limited, Guildford, Surrey

Contents

Acknowledgements

We would like to thank those who have given us permission to reprint extracts from the following plays:

East by Steven Berkoff
Reprinted by permission of Faber & Faber Ltd.

The Caucasian Chalk Circle by Bertolt Brecht
Reprinted by permission of University of Minnesota Press

The Seagull by Anton Chekhov
Translated by Michael Frayn. Published by Methuen. Reprinted by permission of Random House UK Ltd.

A Flea in Her Ear by Georges Feydeau
Translated by John Mortimer. Reprinted by permission of the Peters Fraser & Dunlop Group Ltd.

Abigail's Party by Mike Leigh
Reprinted by permission of the Peters Fraser & Dunlop Group Ltd. on behalf of Mike Leigh

Once a Catholic by Mary O'Malley
Copyright © Mary O'Malley, 1978, reproduced by permission of Amber Lane Press Ltd.

The Entertainer by John Osborne
Reprinted by permission of Faber & Faber Ltd.

Look Back in Anger by John Osborne
Copyright © John Osborne, 1985, reproduced by permission of Faber & Faber Ltd.

The Caretaker by Harold Pinter
Reprinted by permission of Faber & Faber Ltd.

Camino Real by Tennessee Williams
Copyright © 1953, 1954 by Tennessee Williams. Published by New Directions. Reprinted by permission of the University of the South,

We would also like to thank those who have given us permission to print the following photographs:

Antony and Cleopatra, Love's Labour's Lost, Abigail's Party and *Once a Catholic* photographed by John Haynes

The Seagull and *The Caretaker* photographed by Ivan Kyncl

Marat photographed by Chris Parker. By courtesy of the Performing Arts Library

Look Back in Anger photographed by Houston Rogers
From the collections of the Theatre Museum. By courtesy of the Board of Trustees of the Victoria and Albert Museum

1
Let's Talk Sense About Acting

Or, rather, let's try. This book tries to clarify what skills the actor should have, and how to acquire and develop them; it also looks at the processes and thinking that lead to good acting. Acting and the actor have always been shrouded in mystery, and actors have often been regarded as a priestly caste engaged in an activity which is nearly magical. Magic moments do happen in performance – they happen in the hearts and minds of the audience, often we hope. The magic that happens to the actor is when he has a moment of creative insight and knows with all his being that something is right: how to say that line, how to convey that meaning with a look, a smile or a shrug, how to reveal that particular feeling.

Magic apart, most good performances are the result of hard work, deep and sympathetic judgements of humankind, and fine selectiveness. And since acting is mainly a team activity actors are involved in a three-way relationship: with the play or script, with their fellow performers, and with the audience. So the inspirations and intuitions of rehearsal must be refined into a performance, which will be ruthlessly economical, pregnant with meaning, and artistically truthful.

The art and craft of acting has no rules. There is no 'right' way of acting, no particular method and means of using acting skills that will inevitably produce the correct results; besides, who is to judge what is 'right'? The director? The audience? There can be very many different ways of playing Hamlet, with varying emphases on the many aspects of his character, and twenty different actors will give subtly different performances, according to their ideas of his life and character. Yet each gives us an identifiable Prince of Denmark, in a particular situation, at a particular time in history. A production of a play, or the making of a film, is an organic, pragmatic business, the combining of the thoughts of the writer, actors and director: these actors, this text, *now*. The object of the performance should be to create something believable, human, and to make the audience think, whilst they are being amused, moved, enlightened, informed, or scared out of their wits. So the actors try to find a way of conveying the

1

thoughts and experiences of their characters; to do this they need a wide, supple technique, a set of skills, mental and physical, that enables them to convey their understanding of a character and allows a great variety of expressiveness.

In the mainstream of English-speaking acting there are two huge and influential schools of thought, British and American. Both are profoundly influenced by Stanislavsky, that key figure, of whom more later. Briefly, the British dramatic actor is more focused on technique, the American actor more inspirational and mindful of emotion, and its effect on the watcher.

Technique

Technique liberates the actor. Technique is the means by which ideas and feelings are turned into a believable performance. Without expressive skills, the actor is awkward and confused; what he thinks and feels about a part is only the germ of the performance, which must be realised emotionally in terms of speech, use of language, movement and body language. There are four words here which nearly every acting teacher, director and actor use again and again: what? where? why? how? – questions which relate closely to the way in which a character is placed in his or her social and emotional context. How? is probably the most important question for the actor because it affects what you do, how you do it and with what. I will be exploring these things through the book.

Technique takes two forms. When we say an actor has a good technique we mean that he or she has, most importantly, a strong, musical, attractive voice, clear and articulate speech, skill in the use of language and vocal expression. Also a well-managed body, agility, finesse and an expressive use of movement. The actor will have the ability to work creatively, to focus his thought on what he's doing in a deep but economical way, and will be in possession of well-tuned stage skills – a sense of pace, and timing, for example, a sense of size and energy, a sense of style.

The other aspect of technique is the manner in which all of these qualities are brought to bear on *that* particular play, *that* particular script. For example: there's a world of difference between playing the exquisite Gwendolen in *The Importance of Being Earnest* and the lovely Sylv (she of the 'legendary knockers') in Berkoff's *East*. Both girls are much of an age, wanting most of the same things, perhaps having many of the same feelings, and they're not difficult to understand. But they are quite difficult to act. They belong to different tribes and different times and so do things – dress, speak and move – very differently. Gwendolen wears a flowing dress, pretty little shoes and a gorgeous hat; her social class and upbringing show in every move and gesture she makes, she's as complex and artificial as an Oriental princess. Sylv wears towering white stilettos, a very tight blouse or jumper, and a very tight, very short skirt. She's another kind of princess, the princess of the Lyceum Ballroom, and equally complex, speaking a special form of English in a special way. So successful acting of both these girls depends very much on asking what, where, why and how.

Learning Actor's Skills

Can acting be taught? Nobody can teach that essential ingredient, talent, which I'll try to define shortly. Given talent, the actor must be able to express it by acquiring technique, by learning the skills of the performer: command of voice and speech, a feeling for words, movement and body language, and how to think about bringing all these things together.

Voice and speech is still the actor's primary skill. Most of their communication is by the spoken word, and the scripts actors now work with require much greater variety in ways of speaking than they did forty years ago. Yet whatever the mode or style of speech, it must convey articulate sense, and it must be a pleasure to listen to. However, as the actor is also the interpreter of the text, he must develop finesse and subtlety and be highly responsive to his character's use of language. The simpler the human being, the harder it is to speak as that character.

Present day acting is also very visual and makes great demands of the actor's movement skills. The actor may have to represent not only a great diversity of human types, but also things and machines. From *East*, by Steven Berkoff:

> Mike turns Les into a motor bike and jumps on his back using Les's arms as handle-bars. The two clearly create the sound of a motor bike revving up and changing gear during the scene. The strength of the engine as it careers round corners should be apparent.
>
> MIKE: I am a Harley Davidson...

Agility; repose; economy; expressiveness; all qualities an actor needs to convey through the body. He may also find himself working in performances which involve dancing, tumbling and acrobatics.

Quite apart from the physical skills he must acquire, the actor has to develop a level of awareness which amounts to a form of mental training; he has to learn to concentrate, to think and respond creatively, to observe, to recall and recreate emotion in a selective way. He also has to think deeply about a text, to analyse it. Acting is not an intellectual activity, but the evolutionary process of a performance is helped by having learned ways of thinking, of going about things, experimenting. An actor needs to have acquired these ways of thinking and perceiving if he is to find full creative expression in his work. He also has to learn to work with his fellow actors, his text, his director and his audience. He must learn how to rehearse, and about stagecraft. Acting is a very pragmatic business, and what you do has to look and sound right. The audience may not know about the mysteries of acting, but they do know about people and life.

In past times, actors learned their skills simply by *doing it*, undergoing a very long apprenticeship, usually in provincial theatre, since until this century theatre was the only place where acting happened. Nowadays there are many good and successful actors who have hardly ever acted on the stage, confining their work to the cinema and television. Often celebrated older actors pronounce against any form of training except experience itself, though they have in fact received many hundreds of acting lessons from working with talented and craftsmanlike actors and actresses. The art of acting will always be passed on by the fine performers, since other actors will try to emulate them, but there is a great risk that they may merely be imitated. Actors are great because of their talent and individuality, and illustrate vividly how each and every actor, is unique. Modern training emphasises that individuality, and aims to ally it with performance skills.

Most modern actors are highly trained. They earn their living in widely differing media, the size of the stage needing very different techniques from those required by the film or television screen. Most of the professional actors under fifty today would probably have spent three years at drama school (in other countries, especially Eastern Europe, perhaps four or five years) mastering the basic skills and methods taught them by specialists. They will have gained practical experience as a working actor by appearing in a variety of plays under the guidance of professional directors who also have a talent for teaching. The real making of an actor is a process that may take many years; some actors 'come into their own' (as it is comfortingly put) in middle age, especially the intelligent, gifted, but not especially good-looking actor.

Becoming a good actor is a matter of both growing and refining, reflecting an increased knowledge, experience and understanding in performance. After ten years of doing it an actor, amateur or professional, has probably stabilised and improved his or her voice and speech, learned economy of movement and above all repose and stillness, and has found out what he or she is good at. The other important discovery he's probably made is how other people see him, and how this may influence the way in which he is cast. Actors complain bitterly about being 'type cast' but it's a fact of life. However skilled or experienced the actor, there is no reason why he should not continue to polish his skills throughout his working life, by study, practice and taking classes with experts, in much the same way as singers, musicians and dancers do. Over the last thirty years the training of actors has improved greatly, and the mature working actor will nowadays take advice from an appropriate teacher. The National Theatre and the RSC provide workshops in specialist areas and have voice and movement experts on their staff. Laurence Olivier worked for six months with his voice tutor to add two lower notes to his voice in preparation for playing Othello.

Talent

Let's try to define it. Acting talent comes in many forms. Albert Finney's got it, so has Ken Dodd and so has Meryl Streep. A great number of people have some talent for 'acting'. We often use the word to describe manipulative, persuasive or self-dramatising behaviour. True acting talent is distinct from skill in dissimulation, as it is distinct from being an entertaining person, an extrovert or a charmer. Some very good actors are in themselves ordinary-looking and quiet in personality. At the core of talent is an ability to see and understand people and characters from the inside, *from their own point of view*. Actors call this 'getting into the skin of a part'; it's also known as 'empathy'. It's an intuitive ability rather than a pseudo-psychoanalytic process, and the actor must possess it. He must have a gut feeling about what makes a character tick, and a desire to bring that character to life, to recreate his feelings, wants and experiences. The actor must want to show that character to the world, to share him with an audience.

Rich imagination is a part of talent and something which the actor must feed and nurture all his life. Everything in life is food for the actor's imagination. Much of what happens on the stage or screen will never happen to most of us, but the actor must be able to imagine them: death, misfortune, mind-blowing ecstasy; how it feels to belong to another time, another race, another culture. Acting is about recreating existence, a reality that's happening here and now, and having emotions and feelings about it.

The actor suffers and enjoys his character's experiences, and to do so believably must understand his own and other people's emotions, having no inhibitions about expressing the deepest and most private feelings. He or she must also possess the ability to relate to people sympathetically, and sometimes even seductively, in a wide sense. The great actor Coquelin said that acting was like making love to a thousand people a night (I presume he meant simultaneously). Now there's a man who enjoyed his work.

Talent may also include a natural sense of rhythm, in speech and movement, and an instinct for body language, that is, a physical expressiveness which carries meanings beyond those conveyed by speech. An actor can be any shape or size and should have the quality that we call 'watchability' or 'presence'. Ken Dodd is supremely watchable, whilst contriving most of the time to look as silly as possible, brandishing his tatty tickling stick. And an essential ingredient of talent is THE WILL TO DO IT. This is hugely significant and embraces all the following virtues: courage, tenacity, persistence, patience, deep thought, tolerance, optimism and above all, humour.

Let's sum up the definition of talent:

- The gut intuition for seeing people and characters from inside, from their point of view.
- A rich, free-flowing imagination.
- Uninhibited and sympathetic emotionality.
- The will to do it.

With a decent bit of the first, a reasonable amount of the following two, and a great deal of the last, the would-be actor is ready to learn how to be a good actor.

The Actor as Himself; The Actor as Impersonator

There are as many types of actor as there are people, but they tend to lean toward either playing someone very like themselves, in terms of looks, age and personality which sounds easy but isn't, or impersonating somebody quite unlike them: of different physique, age, education, class, temperament, or any of a multitude of personal characteristics. Most 'star' actors belong to the first category; without noticeably changing their appearance, speech, personality and mannerisms they manage to be credible. Bernard Shaw called this phenomenon 'Persuading the Audience that the Character is You'. This kind of actor is generally known as the 'straight' actor, or what the French call an 'acteur'. He or she engages us as a spokesman for ourselves, but braver, more articulate, suffering and enjoying for us. The nature of acting would seem to be first telling a story, and secondly living and being part of that story. A lot of dramatic material needs heroes and heroines to undergo those tests and dilemmas by which mankind defines his life and identity.

At the other end of the acting scale is the impersonator. Seldom himself, adept at disguise, often a brilliant mimic, he's fascinated by externals, speech, motion, physique, and personal mannerisms and habits. He or she sets out to create an entirely original character from scratch, drawing on many different people and amalgamating various qualities and characteristics into one person, or perhaps playing a 'Type', fulfilling popular preconceptions about a certain kind of person. Three characters from 'Oliver' spring to mind: Nancy, the good-hearted whore, Bill Sykes, the brutal ruffian and burglar, and Fagin, the evil Jewish mastermind of a gang of thieves and rogues. All ripe characterisations, drawn by their original creator in great detail, their appearance, speech, emotions, quirks and motives. Even Sykes' dog is characterised, and a right dodgy dog it is too.

These characters, because it's a familiar story and they have been played many times by many actors on the stage and screen, must be created totally anew by the actors who are playing them yet again, deriving suggestions as to personality and qualities from both the novelist (Dickens) and the dramatiser, Lionel Bart. The actor has to reinterpret the role with originality, invention and freshness, as if it had never been acted before. The actor should aim to approach these roles as seriously and with the same imagination as Antony Sher (a truly formidable impersonator) has applied to Singer, Arturo Ui, and Richard III.

Peter Sellers was the impersonator par excellence. Possessing immense talent and intelligence, he looked very ordinary, the man in the street, yet he produced a great gallery of rich and different characters. Two examples of his working method: his wife Lynne Fredericks says that when searching for a character for Chauncey Gardner, the utter nonentity who by mere chance becomes President of the USA in the satire *Being There*, he spent many hours just walking up and down the hallway of his apartment, getting up and sitting down. He said, 'if I can get the walk I can get the character'. The preposterous French-accented English of his best-known character, the bombastic but bumbling Inspector Clouseau ('Ave you a leecence for that Minkey?' to an organ grinder) was, so rumour has it, based on the spoken English of no less a person than President de Gaulle. Shaw, again, calls this kind of acting 'Persuading the Audience that You are The Character'.

Most actors fall somewhere between these two extremes. Every role could be said to need 'characterisation', since there's a lot more to human character than external appearance and mannerisms: intelligence, emotion, imagination, affections, morality, and hopes and fears. The straightest role contains all these. Many straight actors welcome being 'stretched' by playing parts completely unlike themselves, and character actors long to play well-dressed and glamorous people. The delightful Julie Walters spoofed this idea in a sketch in a 1987 Victoria Wood television special. In the crummy pseudo-soap *Acorn Antiques* she played the treasure, Mrs Overall, fearful floral wrap, ghastly wrinkled stockings, grim hairnet teetering across the set with endless cups of tea trembling in her paw. The actress was then seen off-set; she is elegant, dressed to the nines, and looks like a Hollywood Star of the fifties. She is still very funny, but in a completely different way.

To what extent an actor performs as himself or assumes an impersonation is dependent on his own personality, the nature of his talent, and his reasons for acting. The stage gives him much more opportunity to be flexible, to play character parts since stage make-up and costume can give a very different visual and body image, except in small studio theatres. Before the camera, actors are much more likely to be typecast, to play characters who look or sound like they do. As film and particularly television are the actor's bread and butter, the modern actor must have a shrewd sense of himself as others see him. The camera is deeply penetrating and peels away all falsity. It doesn't miss a flicker. Contemporary television with its huge output of drama can match the actor to the character with great precision. There is an actor around to represent all of us, whatever our race, colour, class, education, sexual orientation, size or age. Disabled actors now have their own theatre company 'Graeae', and are invited to appear in films, on stage and television. Nor do they always act disabled people.

That the sort of parts an actor plays can change is usually due to the actor changing, maturing in looks and personality. We all play sons and daughters till we're old enough to play our parents. Careers change and develop as the actor develops. The darkly handsome James Mason, leading man par excellence, in his later work turned out some wonderfully seedy ageing men on the skids, and the patrician Gielgud is still amusing us with a succession of witty, naughty and indiscreet old buffers. The comedienne Beryl Reid developed into a mature actress of sensitivity and distinction, the great zany Jerry Lewis gave a sinister and weighty performance in *The King of Comedy*. There is no age watershed for the actor. At any time of their lives, they have an aspect of humanity to show to an audience. The actor never stops learning.

The Modern Actor

Modern acting skill has evolved over many centuries in the same way that human society has. Actors have always been the interpreters of the dramatist's ideas about the world and the forces and influences that have directed it: people, their beliefs, culture, politics, morals, and way of life. Until the Restoration of Charles II playwrights wrote mainly about those who governed human society, either kings, nobles, or gods, and their effect on the great mass of humankind, managing in this strict framework to make profound comments on the nature of man, his character and motives. The Restoration marked a tremendous change in the actor's role and performance. First, in contrast to the theatre of Shakespeare's time, women were acted by women, with all the real allure of their sexuality; next, the plays of this time, though packing substantial moral clout, were about everyday things, such as sex, money, the manners and modes of the bourgeoisie. Immediately the actor became the voice and epitome of his time, and his performance came far closer to reality. The great actor David Garrick was much remarked upon for the life-like quality of his performances; he seems to have taken Hamlet's advice to the players.

The greatest influence on acting in the last hundred years has been the work of Konstantin Stanislavsky, founder of the Moscow Arts Theatre. The modern actor is his product. He revolutionised the art of acting, and in a lifetime of acting, directing and teaching from the 1890s to the 1930s, set down on paper the what, the where, the why, and especially the how of the actor's performance. He empha-sised rationality and deductiveness as well as instinct and intuition. His object was to produce acting firmly based on reality and truth; the whole of modern changing industrial society, the sweeping developments in politics, education, medicine, science and manu-facture demanded a way of acting that presented an utterly real picture of life as it was now seen and understood. Liberated human-ity wanted to see a true image of themselves down to the finest and subtlest details. The effect has been profound, and acting has been irreversibly changed for the better.

The other commanding influence of this century has been the film and, in particular, Hollywood. Stanislavsky's 'Naturalism' was the right method of acting for the great gallery of real people that the film now portrayed, and the qualities of truthfulness, detail and underplaying are precisely those needed by the present day screen and television actor. This mode of working requires the utmost concentration, clarity of thought and economy. The physical responses and facial expressions arising from intense emotion must be drawn almost in miniature for the close-up or medium shot, and big physical and vocal action in the long shot must be performed with absolute precision. Michael Caine in a deeply informative television programme gave a most telling demonstration of the screen actor's art and skill by enacting a short scene of dramatic and apparently dangerous action, interspersed with a few words of dialogue, using the show's presenter as his fellow actor. By the end of Caine's 'lesson', the presenter, an agile and intelligent fellow, had just about mastered a 20-second scene, and understood the importance of position, speed, body language, business for the camera, and vocal pitch and level.

Acting on the stage has changed greatly during this century. The demands of so many and various styles of theatre, from pantomime to Pinter, mean that the stage actor must acquire a powerful and versatile technique. A play of heroic action and heightened poetic language may be being acted in a theatre seating 70 or 2000. In contrast, a conversational play which requires subtle speech and delicate nuances of body movement may have to be acted in an auditorium for 1500 people. Yet the dramatic effect must be the same, and the actor therefore needs a fine ability to adjust his *scale* of performance, to judge accurately how much? Stage acting is 'projected', that is, the voice, movement and body are conveying a bigger, bolder image than that needed for acting for the camera. Even quiet, shy or withdrawn characters need projection, but it must not be apparent to the audience.

So the modern actor or actress who works for both stage and screen is above all a consummate technician. This wide range of skills is what enables him to cope with two very different forms of acting. The camera requires above all that the actor *thinks* character, emotion, and situation – a flicker of the eyes, the beginning of a smile, may say it all. The stage actor by comparison is using much more energy, and a lot of the time is up and running.

So what can you learn about acting from a book? The answer is – quite a lot. Voice, speech, analysis of text and creating a character are all subjects more amenable to discussion than, say, movement and body management for the actor. You can gain a better understanding of what you need to learn, and how to go about it. During the following chapters I shall often, and at some length, refer to dramatic texts. I use a wide variety of texts, some of them from other centuries, some modern and experimental. Each play needs a different approach; acting is always specific, not general, for it is about particular people in particular situations.

If I often refer to the actor as 'he', it is merely for convenience and brevity, and I hope women readers will know that I am addressing them as well.

2
The Thinking Part
of Acting

Preparation

The first priority of the actor is relaxation. The actor's body and voice are his instruments, which he must keep in tune all his working life, for every performance, every rehearsal, every class or workshop. Acting is a demanding, challenging and scary activity. Tension of any kind impairs performance; it's energy used in the wrong way. As we progress through the following exercises, it will become apparent that being relaxed is much more than being laid-back or casual or dozy. The properly relaxed actor is in a condition of vibrant repose: balanced, elastic, quietly pulsing with the right sort of energy, both mental and physical – rather like a great boxer or tennis player.

It's interesting to note that most therapeutic processes start by inducing in the patient a better sense of physical well-being, which ideally should be generated naturally. Certainly this is essential for the actor; nobody really acts better for taking a pill or a couple of drinks – that's the road of desperation. Acting is a tremendous challenge to the actor, and an act of self-revelation; it requires courage to confront, convince, and woo the audience, and accordingly the body pumps out adrenalin creating the 'fight and flight' reaction, though actors are not allowed to fly! All good actors feel this sense of apprehension, and all bad actors let it turn into either stage fright, or loss of control, so their performance is either wooden or wild. More performances fail because of 'nerves' than for any other reason.

So we must start with the body. If it's properly relaxed and energised, the physical effects of anxiety and fear will be minimal, and the knocking knees, dry mouth and husky voice will not impair the actor's performance, and the voice and body will respond more easily, more economically to the thoughts and objectives in his mind. Every actor should 'warm up' physically, vocally and mentally before working. 'Warming-up' is a bit of a misnomer, and really means loosening up, focusing the energy. There are several ways of doing this, and the actor must find out what works best for him.

Releasing Tension

This series of short exercises is best carried out standing up, weight carried mainly on the balls of the feet, legs slightly apart. You should be lightly and comfortably clad – don't try it in the suit of armour or the corsets and ballgown you wear in Act Three. The object is to loosen and 'twang' the muscles in all parts of the body: to oil the machine and make the joints free, so that the whole body *flows* through the performance.

Shoulders, face and neck
The head speaks volumes, even when the actor isn't speaking. Consider this example:

I sentence you to death.
There is a pause ... the actor's head slowly droops on to his chest. Another pause. He gives a few brief shakes of his head.

Or

Man - Mary! MARY!
She has her back to him. She opens her eyes wide; a smile of sheer delight crosses her face; slowly she turns her head to look at him...

Start with the shoulders. Stretch the arms upward, as far as you can reach, looking upward, then let the arms fall. Repeat this several times.

Shrug your shoulders, raise them as high as you can; hold for a moment, then drop them. Repeat several times.

Roll the shoulders forward in a circling movement, and then roll them backward.

Think of your chest as a heart-shaped balloon with great lifting power. Your feet can hardly stay on the floor. As you float upward let your head fall forward. Let it gently roll round several times, clockwise and anti-clockwise: be careful to do this without force. It often produces a rather nasty crunching noise, so do it gently.

Imagine a strong, slightly elastic cord running down from the top of your head, through your spine, and attached to your bottom vertebra. As the cord is tugged, it very gently lifts your head and straightens your spine: let your head and spine bounce very gently to the easy pull upward. Let the head *float* up without any help from the shoulders. Imagine that slow beautiful music is in the air all round you, constantly changing its direction – listen to it only with your head and ears.

Face
We wear a mask of daily habit upon our faces, which reflects our thoughts, feelings, awareness and self-image. In our daily lives most

of us compose our faces to try to 'look' something we are not: interested, amused, understanding, at ease, adjusting to the situation we find ourselves in. This is rather different from the actor consciously seeking an expression. Yet actors don't make faces; when they do, it's called, unflatteringly, 'mugging'. Clowns and broad comedians often mug, because their storytelling and expression of feeling is on a broad scale, and they must make their effects quickly and strongly. The face, like gestures, must follow thought and emotions, and on both the small and large screen the smallest facial expression seems false unless absolutely appropriate to the feelings which prompted it. Pulling faces is, though, a good way to encourage flexibility and responsiveness, so mug the most horrible and hilarious faces you can (Les Dawson's 'Gurning' is always a favourite). Stretch and purse the lips, inflate the cheeks, screw up your eyes then open them wide, frown fiercely and release it, waggle your jaw, waggle your ears if you can – always a good party trick – try at the very least to get some movement into your scalp. Finally, start to shake your head and let your skin flop around your skull as if it were about to fall off; you won't look very pretty doing it, but you will have a relaxed face.

Arms and hands

'What do I do with my hands?' says the inexperienced actor. From the centre of your chest to the tips of your fingers, gesture arises from thought or necessity – you pick up a suitcase, you describe a petal falling. To relax the arms and hands, swing your arms like a windmill, then slowly and flexibly flap them like a bird, then raise them and let them fall as though through water. Shake your hands like a loose bunch of bananas till your fingers flap. Play the piano with your fingers; rotate your hands from the wrist, clockwise and anti-clockwise (more crunching noises). If this seems to be giving a great deal of attention to the arms and hands, it is because gesture amplifies the words you are speaking and is sometimes a language in itself. And gesture invariably looks spontaneous, except when the actor deliberately plays the phoney gestures of a self-dramatising character. I saw a handsome, well-spoken and gifted Romeo playing a scene of loving, passionate eloquence with clenched fists, the hands undoing what all the rest of him was doing!

The torso

So far, we've loosened up the top of the body, now let's consider the torso, centre of all our movement, and because it contains our breath, centre of our energy. Take a few deep breaths, lowering the diaphragm by letting the tummy stick out, quite naturally don't protrude it or hollow your back. Breathe out quickly. Now a little bump and grind, rotate your hips one way and then the other. Those who are old enough will remember a riotous dance called the twist, where to fast and rhythmic music you rotated the shoulders one way, and the hips and knees the other way. It was wonderful for a flexible torso, if you survived! Standing with your feet a foot or so apart take a deep breath, and stretch up, and as you breathe out, let the top half of the body fall forward from the hips, first hands, then arms, head, shoulders and chest; let the spine gently curl forward. Hang head down for a moment, then as you take in a deep breath, slowly uncurl, and reach up with a catlike stretch. Repeat this a number of times. The object of this exercise is to flex the muscles of the back, to make all the vertebrae of the spine flexible. Do it gently. The major cause of absenteeism from work is 'back trouble', and the spine, main-mast of the whole body, needs careful treatment.

Legs, ankles and feet
Shake loosely each leg in turn. Clench each foot, and release. Swing each leg like a pendulum. Run lightly on the spot, on the ball of the foot. Standing on one leg lift the other a little and rotate the foot from the ankle – more crunching noises. Do the same with the other foot and ankle. Now launch yourself into kicks with each leg; a good kick involves the whole body, even down to the fingertips, it's an explosion of energy. If you watch a fine footballer, his whole body will be as graceful as a ballet dancer, the arms, torso, hips and legs contributing to that moment of perfect balance and energy.

Finally, bounce lightly on the balls of the feet, then change your weight from foot to foot. Stretch up and breathe in once more. Stand still, breathe easily, look around you. With luck you will now be in that condition of 'vibrant repose'. The *Oxford English Dictionary* defines vibrant as 'thrilling' – not a bad state for an actor to be in.

The Actor's Thoughts

Let's look now at the actor's thought processes, what faculties of mind he should develop, and the most useful ways of going about his work.

First, *the actor is a remembering creature*. Not just his lines, moves, and stage business, but remembering everything he or she has seen, heard, experienced, tasted and smelled, and people he's met, loved, hated and been interested in and frightened by. He must remember feelings and emotions, not only his own, but those of other people. This capacity to remember is not too difficult to acquire; it needs only observation, interest and curiosity. It should become the habit of a lifetime.

Good acting is distinguished by originality, the creation of a character that is unique and well-rounded, rather than a mere type, and also by depth of insight into human motives, feelings, actions and behaviour. The actor's observations, experiences and memories are his creative fuel, stored in the subconscious mind; not a huge data bank of facts and details but a great collection of intuitions and understandings. The process is one of unconscious synthesis. To make it all work the actor must develop these faculties and abilities so that all these elements can be brought to light and made use of in performance.

To make it all work, the actor must develop these faculties and he must learn:

- to observe and to concentrate;
- the ability to draw on his reserves of sense memory and emotion memory;
- to find ways of making connections, both between his own feelings, perceptions and experiences and those of other actors, working at both conscious and unconscious levels; to tell stories and to improvise;
- to perceive the intentions of a character, and the obstacles in his or her way.

All of these faculties come into play when creating a performance; they are as much a part of an actor's technique as are skills in speech and movement. The rest of this chapter is concerned with showing ways and means of exploring these matters. The ideas, exercises and improvisations which follow are ways of gaining access to your innermost self – to thought processes, feelings, emotions, memories, conscious and unconscious, so that all these elements can be unearthed and used creatively.

Concentration

Concentration doesn't imply tension, it is *focus*. We tend to call to mind a figure like Rodin's 'Thinker', with body hunched, muscles tense, brow knitted, when imagining a human being concentrating, but concentration is purely a question of thinking only about the matter in hand, whether that is an idea, a feeling, or an area of experience. So all self-consciousness, all irrelevant anxieties, must be banned from the actor's mind. Creating a part is a growing process, a series of mental happenings and discoveries, with one thing leading to another. If you try too hard you will impose the conscious desire to come up with something clever on your subconscious mind. So concentration is a sort of intellectual and emotional economy.

The Word Game – Connections

The word game is used by actors in training to release a spontaneous flow of association of ideas from the subconscious. The temptation is to try to be clever, witty and apt. Resist this, as it's more important to be able to talk nonsense and gibberish, to let one thing lead to another, to remove the constraint of being sensible. The exercise is for two actors or a group. One actor says the first word that comes into his head, the next responds immediately without thinking, with another word, the next actor follows up. Something like this might emerge:

SUNSHINE BRIGHT SNAPPY HAPPY YELLOW GOLDEN COIN CORNY JOKE LAUGHTER MIRTH GIRTH FAT FALSTAFF DRINK DRUNK DROOPY LOOPY FLYING FLOATING DANCING FENCING PINCHING NIPPING NOSE RED RUDE RIDE FLOAT BOAT GLOAT LEER BEER ... and so on.

As self-awareness falls away the actor begins to concentrate in the right way; and the whole process asks the question 'what is in your head that you don't know about or won't let loose?' We invariably tend to edit what we say, even what we think, and want to give an impression of ourselves to others, to compel them to think about us or judge us in a particular way. To act well we must make ourselves free of that desire, which inhibits creativity.

Instead of being an extraordinary instrument that receives, digests and emits what you are is merely a man or woman with opinions, and probably prejudices and defensive self-consciousness.

You mustn't think that in doing such exercises to gain freedom you are surrendering self-control or making a fool of yourself. If you utter something vulgar or violent or foolish, so be it. Ask yourself what brought it out, and you will find some cause, probably outside your work: self-consciousness, the desire to shock your fellow-actors, a private anxiety. Accept that, and consider how it helps you to realise something that has as yet been invisible and unknown.

Storytelling

An actor both narrates, lives and interprets fictions of other people. As such he or she must develop a capacity for telling stories. An audience of adults is full of child-like curiosity, waiting to be emotionally gripped by a tale, by revelations and surprises.

Here is another group exercise, for at least two actors: the object is to explore thoughts and feelings with other people, again feeling toward an indistinct objective. Each actor must let flower in himself a sense of child-like wonder; if this happens, a remarkable newness and freshness of emotion is communicated. And, at another level, a group of actors can create a play by storytelling, and may often have to, when there's no suitable play and no money to pay writers. This can happen from the humblest fringe companies to the sophisticated work of Mike Leigh (whose work we look at in Chapter 4).

Something like this may emerge. (The director's brief in this case was 'Create a Space Thriller'.)

ACTOR A   An astronomer in Southern England is scanning the heavens in a major observatory. Even though it's three a.m. and he's been at work since midnight, the work fascinates him. He's using the newest and largest optical telescope yet built. It's a cold clear November night. To his great excitement he sees, in the constellation Coma Berenices, what he thinks is a new star, a brilliant point of light, and as he watches it he becomes aware that it's getting larger and brighter, and apparently approaching the earth. He reaches for the phone and punches up the two digits for the Royal Observatory... (The next actor takes over.)

ACTOR B   He gets the engaged signal. 'Are the lines jammed, is everyone ringing in?' he thinks. He puts down the phone and returns to the eyepiece. The star now appears much bigger, and there's been an alarming development in the thirty seconds he's been on the phone: the star is accompanied by a spot of intense blue light, slightly ahead of it. The blue sphere has a nimbus of vapour round it...

ACTOR C   He sits back for a moment, thinking, 'am I going crazy? These things only happen in Sci-Fi stories. Is this the result of last night's party? Sonia gave me a bad time, and I'd had too much to drink.' He looks round the observatory, and notes that everything seems normal. 'The hell with it, I'm a trained scientist, I don't *see* things.' He picks up the phone again, and redials the Royal. This time he gets the ringing tone, and the phone is immediately picked up at the other end and a voice says 'Jerry, is that you?' Then silence...

ACTOR D   'Hello, hello! Yes, this is Jerry, but how the heck did you know it was me?' He waits for a reply, when suddenly the number unobtainable signal sounds. As he's about to redial he becomes aware of a low humming sound: trouble in the power unit? He looks up at the great bank of dials and indicator lights to one side, and sees that the power room warning signal is flashing; he turns back to the telescope, and sees that it's vibrating. As he stretches his hand out to touch it the motion stops, but the bare metal is hot to the touch...

ACTOR E   As he looks up at the great glittering machine against a rectangle of velvet-blue sky he sees that the top end of the telescope where the great outer lens is located is surrounded by a halo of intense blue shimmering light, and as he watches the top end of the forty foot tube is being slowly crushed, as if by an immense invisible hand. The silence now is absolute. Suddenly there is a click behind him, and as he spins round he sees the smooth alloy doors to the observation room slowly opening...

ACTOR F   A silver-clad elegant leg snakes round the side of the door, followed by a beautiful girl clad in a tight one-piece suit of some metallic fabric. She carries what looks like a gun. She advances toward the paralysed Jerry, smiles, and says in a low husky voice... 'Hello, Earthman...'

DIRECTOR   Stop! Stop!

Let's just quickly peep into the actor's thinking:

ACTOR A   Science and space fascinate me. The biggest old-fashioned telescope felt like the biggest galleon, or a hundred-foot high warhorse. There are 10,000 galaxies in Coma Berenices...

DIRECTOR   Thanks for giving us such an inspiring start.

ACTOR B   Well, it's not going to go away, is it? I remember as a kid seeing a distant blue light, and it was weird...

ACTOR C   It's pure Hollywood. Where's the human interest? Do you want Michael Caine to play the lead or not? Sonia could be Russian, yes, the girl in silver's got a Russian accent...

DIRECTOR   And silver teeth, like Jaws?

ACTOR D   I'm a machine buff. Our kitchen has everything, they all switch on and off and flash lights. One day it's all going to blow up...

ACTOR E   I got stuck with Fine Writing. How did you like 'great glittering machine'? And the crushed phallus?

ACTOR F   Who is Actress F: God; men are self-important. I thought

19

I'd send it up and make the central character female. You were all like a bunch of schoolkids...

DIRECTOR   Exactly. We can do it for the kids, or sell it as a movie.

A light-hearted look at actors being creative, and connecting with each other. All this work should be done with some lightheartedness, and even rehearsals of the bleakest tragedy should have some laughter in them, to allow everyone to let off steam after all that horror.

Sense Memory

Sense memory is Stanislavsky's term for our recollections of our real sensations and how we react to our sensory perceptions. Sight, hearing, touch, taste and smell are our personal radar. If the actor is doing something special, perhaps it's because he's showing a kind of super-sensibility, feeling, hearing and seeing with more intensity than the ordinary person, even when playing someone who does not appear to be very sensitive. A director friend described this as 'high energy superlife'. I approve of his metaphor, as acting is such a mysterious activity that at times it can only be described in metaphors (and an actual account of what actors do would make us summon the men in white coats).

We must train and refresh our use of sense memory. It's an instrument that helps us to create the physical world of a character. The actor playing King Lear must recall many sensations: Lear is hungry, he is cold, he stands in pouring rain, in wind, in darkness, he is assailed by thunder and lightning, he feels immense fatigue, he feels the weight and frailty of his own body; the actor is conveying Lear's realisation, perhaps for the first time, of what it is to be mortal. Without a powerful sense of physical reality he is nothing, merely an actor speaking wonderful language against a background of effects.

Being human is very much to do with sensory reality, and these things have power to move us: a starving beggar tears at the food he is given, and we eat and rejoice with him, a drunken glutton stuffs yet another choice morsel into himself, belches, and we are moved to disgust and anger. A freed prisoner steps out into the day, blinks and weeps at the light, and inhales the fresh air as if it were wine. He has been used to semi-darkness, to the stink of bodies, dirt, dust, excrement, harsh disinfectant. He rubs his wrists, he tentatively stretches his limbs, savouring the feeling of not wearing fetters.

Find time to experiment with states of being. Sit relaxed and close your eyes, and remember from your own experiences everything you can about what it is to see, hear, touch, taste and smell. Don't forget, the special quality of the actor is to give depth and intensity to the most ordinary experiences. In Western urban society we are surrounded by a multitude of sensations: noise, industry, music, screen images, traffic, advertisements, foodstuffs – dazzle, scream, stink and seduction. So pick your subject for contemplation and concentrate. Here are some suggestions for sensory experiences on which you might focus:

You're sitting at a garden table, freezing cold, no gloves, no hat. A friend brings you a steaming hot cup of coffee and a woollen bonnet. Pull on the bonnet, down over your frozen ears, warm you frozen fingers on the mug, smell the steam rising from the coffee.

A beautiful person walks slowly towards you. Remember the rhythm of their movement, the smile on their face. They bend down and kiss you. Smell their scent and feel the touch of their lips.

We react physically to space. Imagine you are in a wide and beautiful landscape, at rest, just looking at it, its soothing colours, balmy atmosphere, sense of peace. Now remember confinement, claustrophobia, darkness; remember the most uncomfortable place in which you've ever been.

Recall the activity you do with the most ease and pleasure: it may be dancing, swimming or walking, but try to remember the pleasure of an exuberant activity. Remember the nature of objects, the differences of texture between silk, leather and coarse wool. Think about the pleasant sensuous texture of, say, a beautiful piece of clothing, and compare it with a repulsive and filthy set of rags.

In your memory, recall sounds, music and voices, the most frightening sounds and the most pleasing. Remember a piece of music that has the power to make you weep.

As civilised people we like to think that we have a great ability to respond to our environment, but it is very probable that we shut things out and look away from what is repugnant to us, and uncritically indulge in that which gives us pleasure. And this shows in performance, when an actor sees but doesn't hear, touches but doesn't taste. Acting for the camera, which takes in every detail, needs absolutely truthful evidence of the senses.

Emotion and Emotion Memory

This is another of Stanislavsky's terms. Acting is about human feeling, understanding, or trying to understand, and if this is not communicated to the audience then the performance is wasted. It is in the very nature of acting that playing emotions, of whatever kind, whether they be light or profound, must be an accurate *simulation* of feeling. The actor on stage or in front of a camera has many tasks to perform, and he cannot risk being overwhelmed or out of control, which comes across as self-indulgence, something the audience and critics can easily spot. How people express emotion is conditioned by a lot of factors, of culture, race, class, age, intelligence, hormones, situation, and above all individual personality. So, to a large degree the actor can only play what is within his or her emotional compass though each should work to expand it. There are no standards for emotion, and depth of feeling and expression of feeling are different for every human being. Many years ago it was a prerequisite for the student in the final stage of drama school to learn to act 'hysteria', that is, to progress from tears to laughter, or laughter to tears within a short speech or scene. This is a difficult thing to accomplish and many fine actors and actresses not only can't do it, but won't. They can, though, endow a character with infinitely subtle shades of feeling of a less dramatic nature. Some actors are natural 'waterworks' performers, and can sob movingly at 10 o'clock on a Thursday morning, precisely on cue. The actor's emotional integrity lies in acute and sympathetic observation of feeling, and in brave and well-controlled demonstrations of how it is shown. Your own deepest experiences of emotion must at some stage in rehearsal be transmuted into finding ways in which you can convey your characters emotions: what did she do? What happened to her? How was she affected? How did she speak? What was her energy level? How was she affected physically? How fast did she think? An actor playing a character who is suffering distraught and anguished will not be feeling thus in performance, nor would an actress playing the first night of a comedy, wherein she is charming, light-hearted and frivolous, be feeling so before she begins her performance. She's going to grit her teeth, do her relaxation, honour the contract she has with the play, her fellow-actors and the audience, draw all her skills together, swish on, and give every *appearance* of having a wonderful time.

So we see that we are looking at the understandable, recognisable *effects* of emotion: what the feeling has engendered, which is unique and personal. The actor in rehearsal must experience the emotion, try to create it from his or her own experience, or imagination: and allow that feeling to produce its effects on body, voice, mood, demeanour. Some of the time the actor may be aware of what it's doing to him, and at other times the reaction of his fellow actors, or the director's feedback will reveal what actually happened. So there is a positive use in recreating emotion in rehearsal, to dig into one's own experience, or to imagine an experience equally affecting. Juliet may find it difficult to imagine having a lover die, she might find Romeo unattractive, but she might remember the anguish and tears at eleven years old when her beloved spaniel died. This useful process is *transference* of emotion, letting one set of emotional feelings and their expression, stand in for something much graver. An observant and sympathetic actor can derive great knowledge of emotional behaviour and its causes simply by keeping his eyes and ears open, by listening to the distress and delight of his friends, by watching people enjoying themselves, and above all by trying to understand WHY.

The British are very cautious of displays of untoward emotion, the middle classes in particular. At its most absurd level this reticence is typified by 'the stiff upper lip', something of a caricature these days since British society is now more diverse than ever, broadened by influences and cultures from Asia, Africa, the Caribbean, Australia and Canada, and the influence of the Jewish people. I said 'untoward' emotion, because I believe that contemporary British acting most often walks the tightrope between true and moving feeling and demonstrative self-indulgence with great skill. I hope my American readers won't be offended if I say that at times some American acting seems over-emotional. Certainly some of the philosophies of actor training appear to emphasise the need for the outpouring of instantly accessible feelings at any price, as though *emotionality* was the main criterion of honest and moving acting. I have this feeling not, I hope, out of chauvinistic prejudice, but from many years of enjoying superb American acting with a critical eye, and having participated in the training of many fine young American actors. Having said this, American actors have much easier access to sheer charm, fun, panache, and by comparison we can seem heavy footed and ungiving. Perhaps the difference is that English as spoken by the British actor does a bit more in conveying emotional meaning – feeling is expressed through language alone. For the good of acting in English, vive la différence.

Let's now examine improvisation, the actor's chief way of exploring his subconscious and emotions, a means of dissolving inhibitions, and a tool to help the actor make connections.

Improvisation

Improvisation is acting from moment to moment, without a dramatic script and without any deadlines. It has often been treated as a party game, a version of charades, where actors feel compelled to invent dialogue, or make dramatic effects: this merely makes the actor feel uncomfortable. The real use of this all-encompassing exercise is to explore the imagination, release intuition, and help the actor to find that there is a part of the acting process that is beyond the conscious, beyond obvious reasoning, what Marlon Brando's biographer describes as 'moments beyond technique'.

Improvisation is a skill in itself and a vital part of the actor's technique, lying at the heart of actor training, but it must be used in the right way: any conscious attempt to manipulate the moment, the happening, puts a shutter down on the very object of the work. The object is exploration of character, relationships, situations, but above all of the actor himself, his *un*conscious knowledge, memories, and emotions. It enables him to liberate himself from his inhibitions, his attitudes and prejudices, his conscious intelligence and judgements. It's a time when the actor can develop himself, unfold his deeper feelings and thoughts without a duty to the audience or the dramatist. There is no endproduct in dramatic terms, and no success or failure. Things may emerge from improvisation that are later incorporated into performance, for example, discoveries about the area being worked on, information that's been discovered, attitudes and understandings that have changed. Sometimes it's valuable to improvise during rehearsal, playing the characters and situation in some depth in a few very small parts of a scene without using the dramatist's dialogue, perhaps varying the action, though this is only useful when an actor is 'stuck', and reasoning, discussion, and rehearsal have failed to develop the scene.

How to Use Improvisation

The work needs an observer, who may be the director, acting teacher, or a fellow-actor who has common sense and can watch astutely. He or she will advise the actors on what emerged during improvisation with clarity, humanity and insight. You need to know several things before starting: where are we? What point of what situation have we reached? What relationship do the characters have to one another? And most important of all, *what does my character want?* This is sometimes known as the 'objective' or 'motivation', and has two levels, what the character wants in the long-term, the life-plan, and what the character is trying to achieve immediately. These objectives are the mainspring of all character, and all acting. (Sometimes this 'want' can be very difficult to grasp: Christopher Hampton's comedy *The Philanthropist* has a central character whose principal want is to agree with everybody and to lead a life devoid of emotional friction or involvement.)

Generally, the information given to the actors is spartan, and the objective of each character simple, that is, 'what do I want now, at this moment?' You might be one of a Pools syndicate who've just heard of a huge win, or a minority group in a despotic country who are facing exile or worse. Whatever the situation may be, the actor must feel free to speak or not, move or not, and must not make any attempt to 'write' a clever scene. There are many facile and shallow actors who can create reams of banal dialogue, and very good actors who are sparing with words. If you pursue your objective, something will happen, and the actor, as in life, may struggle for words or find them easily. The same must apply to emotion and feeling: *let it happen* from what occurs in the course of the improvisation, the pursuit of wants, the problems and difficulties that arise from the situation, the discoveries made about relationships. Other characters may have a completely different set of priorities.

The objective may change as the improvisation develops. If your objective is to cheer up a friend who is apparently unhappy, and he reveals that he has committed a serious crime, your response may veer from offering comfort and help on a superficial level to one of uncertainty: should you help? Can you help? His life and freedom are in the balance. Maybe the crime is so abhorrent that your objective becomes, 'let me get out of here'. Maybe his crime is most shameful, and you find yourself reacting with prurient curiosity, or panic, covering your ears to block out his confession.

Improvisation is a garden where all aspects of human behaviour and responses, may grow, and the painful or shameful inevitably arise. Only say what you mean, which may even take the form of a lie or dissimulation. Don't ACT. If you do, the work will be stagey and false and you won't get to a deeper understanding of truth and reality. ('Truth' and 'reality' are now almost clichés of pretentious actor-speak, but their depth and presence marks good acting from bad.) Believe in your objective, believe in the other characters, and let your emotions arise out of what happens between you, or from the situation itself. Through the frequent use of impro the actor learns to *focus* and select, to concentrate on what drives the character, and to contemplate his own resources of emotion, imagination, and access to sense and emotion memory. It reveals you to yourself, and points the way to areas of development and release: 'I'm still very scared of being at a disadvantage', 'I jump about and get over-excited by the idea', 'I *do* too much' are the thoughts that can emerge. These are all pointers toward a necessary self-understanding

– and the actor *must think of himself* with understanding and sympathy, in order to meet the challenge of difficulties, working for strength and flexibility in areas where he's weak: a career in acting is one of continual adaptation.

Some Subjects for Improvisation

Work falls roughly into two areas: the general, where the idea may be to dig into states and conditions of which we may have no experience. Here the actors are inventing, freeing their memories and intuitions. The other area is concerned with the specific, with a very particular situation or relationship, and the subtleties or extremities of emotion it reveals. In every case the intention is to work beyond the cliché, to find something deeper emotionally and expressively. Consider in the first area a group of actors working on the subject of old age: what better than to improvise a group of elderly people enjoying, or perhaps not enjoying, a meal together. The first thing the actor should do is sit down, and pick up an imagined knife and fork or a spoon; or perhaps it's a tribal society with different customs, who eat with their fingers from a communal dish. The most important catalyst of an improvisation is *instinctively doing*. Action. Even if it's only reaching out an arm. Speak if you have a reason for speaking: 'Do have some of this', 'pass the mustard,' 'more wine,' 'I don't like fish'. All words are associated with action, with human contact or rejection; the old woman who doesn't like fish sits with her arms folded: the actress has seen fish on a plate in front of her, and reacts like a child, pursing her lips and repeatedly shaking her head. The actor who says pass the mustard has let roast beef float into his mind. He likes roast beef, he has had no breakfast before class, and it's midday, so going with his own hunger, he eats greedily, clumsily and noisily. He reaches out for more, but all the beef has gone. Obstacle. He looks aggrieved, and looks round at the plates of the other eaters. Again, the child emerges. The actor who helps someone else to food or drink might be exhibiting either the desire of the old to please, or at least not to offend, or be rigidly adhering to a code of gentlemanly manners of fifty years ago. One actor has a denture, she's had it since the age of twenty-seven, so any discomfort and inconvenience it might cause her when eating is uppermost in her mind. She knows the difficulty of the tiresome prosthesis, so cuts up her meal with great care and eats with concentration, slowly and carefully, saying little. What she wants, food, is set against two problems, false teeth and the need to preserve her dignity. Two intentions, two obstacles.

The key to starting this creative investigation is to physicalise the characters' world, the people and places and objects that it contains. An actress may look up at the dingy curtains of the rehearsal room and sigh: something in her mind is saying 'is this what it's going to be? Less? Worse?' Transfer the actors to the kitchen, where they clear the plates and dishes, pots and pans, another and more strenuous area of activity; taps are difficult to turn, slippery dishes difficult to handle, retrieving a dropped spoon from the floor involves bending or stooping. What seems to emerge from this improvisation is that activity is reduced, and the world of the old people is circumscribed, which in some cases means there's less to talk about, and trivial daily things take on a greater importance: health, family, comforts are more important perhaps than politics, travel, fashion, or progress.

When we improvise like this we are discovering the truth about a world to which we don't belong, and probing its *realities* and *details*, down to an old man's crumpled handkerchief or the way an elderly woman applies her lipstick. It's a slow, patient process that helps the actor toward depth and subtlety in defining character, and should be combined with the actor's research: observation, photographs, biography, film, recorded interviews, the music and popular literature and press of the period, clothing and amenities. All the actor's concentration and feeling is focused on truth and the real world. There are very few areas of human experience that don't bear profound examination: family life; religion and religious observance; social status and social behaviour; the effect of a particular climate or environment; political or patriotic conduct, and those who dissent from it; work, occupations and trade; close-knit groups with their own mysteries and processes, like soldiers, fishermen, or nuns; nationality. An interesting example of the last theme is the accent and mode of speech invented by the original cast of *The Royal Hunt of The Sun*. Since almost nothing was known of the Inca speech, the cast and their voice coach had to create a credible native accent through improvisation which all the Inca characters could use. The actor is not only working for himself in improvisation, it's a shared experience, of benefit to all, and something he says or does may trigger off another actor.

An improvisation of this nature should be allowed to take its course, since if the actor feels under any pressure to produce results, superficialities of expression, thought and feeling will be all that emerges. Truthful action, speech, and the gradual evolution of relationships is the aim, and if the actor gets stuck in the stagey and obvious the objectives of his character should be changed until he feels free to be creative. The blocked actor can ask himself several questions:

- Do I understand what my character wants? (objective)
- Am I being emotionally honest, or am I trying to make an effect, hiding feeling, or trying to manipulate myself or others?
- Am I watching and listening to the other people, with a belief that they and their feelings are real?
- Am I tense or anxious?
- Am I concentrating and interested?

With more specific subjects for improvisation, the intention is to open out the actor emotionally. We all have areas where we would prefer to be reticent, or where we feel we express ourselves inadequately. In the young actor these are quite likely to be in the area of positive emotion: love, affection, humour, understanding, tolerance and sociability. Since acting is often rather frightening it's easy for the actor to overplay the negative emotions, which can topple over into self-indulgence. (I've tried to illustrate this pitfall by looking at a scene from *The Seagull* in Chapter 4.) To play a scene of highly-charged emotion with another actor requires mutual sympathy, respect and humour; each actor needs to be sure of the other's support, confident they will not be in competition. For the actor in training, all kinds of situations between people should be improvised, so that he or she can find how they respond to them, how easily they can draw on emotion memory, how well they can relate to others. Try to make eye contact and physical contact where it's appropriate. Again, you must know your objective:

- I want to deceive them.
- I want to make love to her.
- I want them to go away/stay here.
- I want to make them laugh.
- I want to put him down.
- I want to praise her.
- I want to reassure him.
- I want us to enjoy ourselves.
- I want to smooth things over.
- I want to regain her trust.
- I want to put him wise.
- I want to get to the bottom of this.
- I want to tear him off a strip.
- I want their respect.
- I want to cry on his shoulder.
- I want to hurt her.

- I want to humiliate him.
- I want to get to know them.

These are just a handful of the multitude of motivations, objectives and reasons for action. The other actor or actors in the scene will have their objectives too. Treat the obstacles which arise as would happen in everyday life, as the solution must be a real solution, not a piece of theatrical outsmarting. A relationship growing in an improvisation is as real as a conversation. The very experienced actor may be disinclined to use this technique, since he has developed a profound intuition and skill in working with other actors, but he should certainly be willing to use it on a younger actor's behalf, or as a contribution to an exploratory project. Improvisation is at the heart of the modern actor's work, as most contemporary cinema, television and theatre is consistently reflecting on, illuminating and explaining life as it actually is.

Let's summarise what the actor needs to bring together, to synthesise in his mind, in order to express himself most fully in his work:

- Imagination – a mind full of images and impressions, gained from his observations and interest in the world.
- The ability to tell a story. This needs a retentive memory, and to acquire this takes practice.
- Understanding of emotion, your own and other people's.
- The ability to remember feelings, and have the courage to express them; the actor's integrity is revealed in the true expression of emotion.
- Delight in the five senses, seeing, hearing, touching, tasting and smelling; remembering the effect of those sensory experiences, and all that is associated with them.
- Mental freedom: the ability to improvise, to explore the unconscious, and to make unconscious connections, to let one thing lead to another.
- A sympathetic and understanding view of other actors, and the characters they are playing: a willingness to relate.

Much of this type of mental activity is spontaneous; though if this is to happen, the actor must be relaxed, physically and mentally.

Everything is grist to the actor's mill, both his own experiences and other people's lives. All art forms are useful, so try to understand how other creative artists make use of sound, rhythm, shape, colour, image and metaphor, music of every kind, poetry and literature. All actors should appreciate language, and not merely the language of the fortunate and well-educated. Performance skills can be mastered with hard work and enthusiasm, but the source of the actor's greatest skill is in his head. That's where his creativeness, imagination and humanity are housed.

3
Voice, Speech and Language

The actor on the stage does most of his work by speaking. He does much less in film and television – a screenplay uses more varied visual and physical images, and contains only about a quarter or even less of the dialogue of a stage play. Different vocal techniques are used in working for the camera, but they are only variations on the actors' basic vocal skills; in spite of much more adventurous use of movement in contemporary theatre and television, the modern actor must be more skilful in the use of his voice than ever before. He must be able to move easily from stage to screen and back if he's going to earn a living.

Contemporary drama covers the whole spectrum of humanity, and is much richer in its exploration of the dialects, modes of speech and vocabularies of people from all classes, the educated and the uneducated. Yet only a few decades ago an upper-middle class accent was essential for English actors, if they didn't want to spend their working lives playing servants or token proletarians; heroes and heroines, Daddy's Girl, and young men coming through French windows carrying tennis rackets all had the same absurd, quacking, affected accents. A long hard look at British films of the 1930s, 40s and 50s reveals a preoccupation with values, and speech to match. An actor with an authentic regional accent had to learn to speak like most of the other actors. That fine, brawny actor John Laurie, best remembered by most people as the lugubrious undertaker Fraser in *Dad's Army*, in his long and distinguished career played many parts in an English accent, including the appalling Duke Ferdinand in *The Duchess of Malfi* and King Richard the Third. When interviewed late in his career, after he'd become famous on television he said he no longer wanted to act in any accent but his own native Scots. Fair enough. If an actor has an authentic way of speaking in addition to standard southern English, he has more strings to his bow: the 'soaps' demand absolute authenticity in Lancashire, Yorkshire, Cockney or wherever they are set, which is just about everywhere. Yet all the schools of drama in Britain, from Bristol to Glasgow teach what is known as 'R.P.', Received Pronunciation. This is educated southern English speech, the language of the communicators. Newsreaders and airline pilots use it, and foreign students of English aim for it. Its virtues are that it's the simplest mechanical way of making the sounds of English speech, it's musical and good to listen to (not that some dialect English isn't), and is understood by the greatest number of people. The classical repertoire, that body of plays of acknowledged excellence, from Shakespeare to Congreve, Shaw and Wilde are usually acted in southern English, though some years ago when John Dexter did a most interesting production of Thomas Heywood's Jacobean tragedy *A Woman Killed with Kindness*, the minor aristocrats and upper classes mainly spoke broad Yorkshire.

Voice, speech and language are mankind's chief intellectual and emotional tools for informing, relating, identifying, manipulating, controlling and even seducing, and the actor needs the utmost skill in their use. Quite simply, whatever kind of actor you are, the audience must want to listen to you. This is not to suggest that acting is a display of the 'voice beautiful', but that the individual actor develops his own unique voice, his ability to use language fully and beguilingly and above all to make sense of what he's saying. So let's look at voice and speech, what they consist of, and how to train and develop them. Voice is the sound itself, speech the form, shape and meaning we give to that sound.

Voice: the Power Supply

The most elementary failure in acting is inaudibility. Even the stars are heckled if they can't be heard. The commonest cause of inaudibility is running out of breath. Breath is the source of all the actor's energies, vocal and physical, and an audience is unconsciously aware of it.

Think of this little scene: a huge wrestler is prowling round his opponent; his movements are smooth and fluid; he's breathing deeply and rhythmically, and his arms are extended, his fingers slowly opening and closing. His opponent is on the canvas, on his back. He has received a colossal head-butt, and his solar plexus is heaving up and down as he fights for breath. The referee is counting. The prone man staggers to his feet, moving uncertainly. There is a pause, and we see the big man draw himself up as he draws in an immense breath, then with a tremendous roar he launches himself on his victim, who screams 'No! NO!' as he hoists him into the air, holds him above his head, then hurls him down on his back again. As he hits the canvas a great gasp bursts from him, and the crowd shrieks, shouts or gasps. Another pause, the winner draws another great breath, the crowd do the same, with another roar he pins his opponent down. The referee has already drawn a big breath, and begins to count 'ONE-er! TWO-er! THREE-er!' in referees' penetrating singsong... The crowd erupts. I've dramatised this little scene in exactly the way good professional wrestlers do. All the drama, all the tension, all the timing, indeed most of the characterisation of the three principals here comes from the way they are breathing (plus suitably barbaric and funny costumes). It is a scene of minimal dialogue, where breath is very life and existence and power, for the wrestlers, the referee and the crowd.

The actor's breath and voice mirror his physical state and his emotional condition. Speech and the use of language reflect his thoughts and intelligence. Most actors have experienced the effects of nervousness, and croaked and husked their way through the first part of a scene. Experienced actors are to be seen standing in the wings, breathing slowly and deeply, so that their diaphragm and hence their breathing is under control. The actor, like the athlete, works continuously to have that extra breath, and to be able to control it as skilfully as a singer or a pearl-diver. Yet the audience or the camera must not see him breathing. Singers, on the stage or the concert platform, tend to wear clothing that drapes comfortably across the torso so that the movements of the diaphragm and solar plexus are hidden. The actor has to do innumerable other things whilst ensuring an adequate supply of breath, so the process must be practised until it is completely instinctive. All breathing exercises should be preceded by relaxation.

The chest and the diaphragm

To have enough breath we need to make the best use of the chest cavity. If you want to make an assessment of what your capacity is, take as comfortable a deep breath as you can, without pushing your chest out, sticking out your abdomen or heaving up your shoulders. Start counting aloud in a normal audible speaking voice. Probably the last few numbers will emerge in a forced gasp, the actor running out of breath. A clear count up to fifty is what to aim for. The director Tyrone Guthrie said that someone who wants to be a classical actor should be able to speak about eight lines of dramatic verse in one breath, obviously without rushing it. One thing that may have happened is that you're breathing out between words, wasting breath. If you want an example of economy when breathing, think of a swimmer doing the crawl: every bit of breath must fuel his energy, and breathing out must be rapid and precisely timed to that moment when his mouth and nose are above the water.

The actor must breathe both with the chest, by expanding the rib cage, and with the diaphragm, the horizontal muscular wall between the chest cavity and the abdominal cavity. We cannot consciously control it, except by relaxing the abdominal muscles; when we do this, the diaphragm drops, and the capacity of the chest is increased. So we have two ways of breathing in and out, the first by letting the rib cage expand outwards, *not* upwards. This we can liken to the opening of a pair of bellows. If at the same time the abdomen relaxes, and protrudes slightly we are in effect lowering a piston, the diaphragm. This process is called 'rib reserve' breathing. It needs to become a reflex action, which requires continual practice. All exercises to develop actor's skills need patient and positive work, in the same way in which experienced musicians, singers and dancers keep their skills in constant health.

Try this exercise when properly relaxed. Stand up, check that your posture is upright without either tension or sloppiness. Put one hand flat on your lower ribs, the other on your solar plexus. Take a deep breath, and feel the rib cage expand automatically and the abdomen protrude slightly; if it doesn't let it go, flexing the stomach muscles to release them. Repeat the earlier counting exercise, raising the diaphragm by gently pulling in the abdominal muscles: this is pushing the piston up to expel the breath. When you've gone as far as you can *without discomfort*, continue breathing out by lowering the rib cage, or rather letting it lower itself, a process rather like a bellows closing. The transition from abdominal breathing to rib reserve must be smooth and effortless, without any unnecessary muscular tension, or change of posture. The audience will have no idea how hard the actor has worked to gain this extra breath capacity; they'll just enjoy listening to him speaking well with good supported tone. You now need to experiment some more with the breathing process. Start speaking softly and then get louder – a lot of dramatic speech has the stress, the emphasis or the meaning at the end. Typical of this is the comedian's joke with its tag or punch-line; here's Archie Rice, John Osborne's clapped-out comedian in *The Entertainer*,

> Here! Here! Here, I've just met a man with a lemon stuck in his ear! A lemon stuck in his ear! So I went up to him, I said: 'What are you doing with that Lemon stuck in your ear?' and he says: 'Well, you know that man with a hearing aid – well, I'm the man with the lemonade.'

An awful gag, but it takes as much skill to play it as a good one.

Try this: take a full breath, and say Hah! with some force, still with the hands in place. If you say it by lowering your rib cage the sound isn't as clear, as rapid, as strong as it can be when you propel it from the diaphragm. Try it again, this time punching it out by a quick pull-in with the solar plexus. Now follow-up Hah! by immediately taking a quick breath, to replace the breath you've used, releasing the tummy muscles. During all this, the rib cage need not have moved at all. This is called a 'snatched breath', and must be rapid and sound-less. The actor breathes without showing it, without lifting the head, arching the back, or raising the shoulders. As the timing and pace of dramatic text is indicated only by the punctuation used, there are often long passages broken only by a comma; here, to sustain what may be a rapid passage, the snatched breath becomes essential. 'Breathing' the dialogue, finding when to breathe to facilitate the speaking of the text is something the actor can work out in rehearsal, or even before when studying a long speech, so that he never runs out of breath.

Now vary the exercise using the words Hoo Hee, punching them out quite loudly, and again voicing them quite softly, but using only your diaphragm. You'll probably manage five to six times loudly, ten to twelve times softly. Nearly all work on the basics in voice class involve repetition and variation of single sounds and combinations of sounds, most of which sound quite inane without the framework of actual words. The purpose is to make the sound correctly every time, and acquire agility and ease with voice and speech. Now try to vary the duration of the word. Say 'WHAT ... ARE ... YOU ... SAYING?' slowly, loudly and deliberately, and try to feel the transition from using the diaphragm pushing up, to the rib cage slowly closing in, not down.

The actor must find out how his body works, and teach it to function easily. A big chest is no guarantee of good breathing capacity, and a lot of notable runners have been markedly skinny, but lithe and flexible with a large chest expansion. The actor who means business should try to find time every day for breathing and speech work, as it takes time and practice to work on the flexibility of the diaphragm and develop particular muscles. Every actor should have his favourite voice book to hand, Cicely Berry, Clifford Turner, or whoever he feels most useful. (See the booklist, p. 179.)

Attack

The aim of developing breathing is to have a big fuel supply, and to be able to deliver it without tension, movement or fidgets or effort. The dual use of chest and diaphragm means that the actor has the tools to use what is called 'attack', which in the exact sense means the precise conjunction of thought, breath, note of the voice and the right position of tongue and lips. It usually means starting bang on in a louder, clearer and more energised voice – King Henry the Fifth at Harfleur, for example:

ONCE MORE unto the breach, dear
friends, ONCE MORE!

I've capitalised once more both times, and added an exclamation mark because it's a great rallying cry, it's bursting with energy and purpose, and could not possibly merely be spoken – nor should it be screamed or shouted. It's cried out loudly and powerfully, since the uproar of war, screams and cries, shouts, clashes, the roar of cannons, is going on at the same time. Particularly in Shakespeare and his contemporaries the actor may have to 'attack' many times; it's heightened poetic language, and needs a powerful and well-controlled voice.

Finally, breathing should be instinctive and effortless, since even quiet speech needs a lot of breath. Richard Burton, who was an exceptionally gifted vocal actor, played his opening scenes as Hamlet in a very low voice, sometimes not much more than a heightened whisper, yet the lines were vibrant with power and danger. This quality is known as 'intensity', which does not mean tense stridency, but rather using a lot of breath to say something with great passion, or quietly and under strong control. All the great film villains use this trick, particularly Brando's Godfather, whose low smoky speech had one big meaning underneath: danger. All intake of breath must be rapid and silent, except when it's part of character. (The hilarious David Jason, a master comedy actor, can be funny merely by breathing or making vocal noises which you can't really describe as speech: his Skullion, the aged university porter, Del Boy, and Pa Larkin made as many noises as they uttered words, and demonstrate how the way a character breathes can be made a feature of characterisation.) Find time to work every day if possible on different samples of dramatic speech, from Shakespeare to modern naturalistic dialogue, to develop the instinct when to breath and how to do it fully and easily. Don't forget that you are the whole actor, and that breathing is related to health, body posture, relaxation and state of mind. When you draw in a breath, you switch on a superb machine but like no other machine, it *lives*. So to the vibrant repose of relaxation we can add Turbine running. The same excitement as on a film or video take when the cameraman says 'CAMERA RUNNING'.

Tone – Trumpet or Flute?

Tone is the quality of the sound you make, the timbre of the voice, its individual and characteristic identity. It can be vibrant and resonant or husky, or clear and musical. Compare Kenneth Williams, with his ringing orotund tone, plumminess used for comic effect, with John Hurt's emotion-laden huskiness, suggestive of past and future pain. It's part of the actor's personality, a sort of vocal fingerprint. A good or interesting tone is persuasive and seductive – witness lots of low-voiced lovers, male and female, in film after film. At the other extreme, soppy or risible characters in sitcoms have adenoidal voices as if they had 'a code id the dose' or are swallowing a dead toad. Oafs and harridans have harsh roaring, muffled or croaking tones. We know that a voice can charm perhaps more than obvious physical attractions, and conversely, are equally aware of the utterly ravishing bimbos or hunks who, when they open their mouths, sound like a chainsaw or a flat tyre.

You are born with a tone, or you grow up into it; it is dependent on the size and nature of the resonators, the cavities where the sound which is made by the vocal cords, vibrates. These cavities are the pharynx (that is the throat), the mouth and the nasal and sinus cavities. The breath excites the vocal cords, and the sound gains resonance in these spaces; we then transform that sound into speech by articulation of vowels and consonants. The voice must be correctly 'placed', that is, the progression of breath to word is smooth and unimpeded by any distortions of the means of production. Two simple experiments will demonstrate wrong voice placement.

1 Speak a few lines of dialogue with your jaw closed, but lips open. The result will be nasal and woolly.

Now check that the jaw is open and relaxed. Voice and speech teachers used to use an unhygienic device called a 'vowel prop,' a small notched piece of bone that was placed between your front teeth to ensure that the volume of the mouth as a resonator stayed constant. The depth of you own thumb is as good a guide as any.

2 Speak the same few lines in as deep a voice as you can, try to use a 'chest' voice. It will probably be a harsh gravelly sound, because you've tucked your chin in and stuck your chest out.

What's happened here is that the pharynx, another resonating cavity, has been distorted. It's like stuffing a rolled-up sock in the bell of a trumpet, or bending a flute. Finally, speak again, pinching your nostrils, which will produce a comic unrecognisable honk.

You can best improve tone by getting all the resonators fully open and relaxed, using the exercises for head, neck, face and torso in Chapter 2, by using the breath economically, not being over-loud, and by articulating clearly. So work to eliminate any tension or distortion of position in the spine, chest, shoulders, neck, jaw and face. Take care, too, of your most important instrument, avoiding extremes of cold, heat or dryness. Avoid infections and colds. Singers always wrap up their throats in cold weather. Try not to smoke too much which is most harmful to the tone and the larynx. Chew gum, which will at least give you a mobile jaw.

The Music of the Voice: the Note

Like timbre, the range of notes of the voice is a natural endowment. We tend to use too few notes when speaking, though spoken educated English has moved a long way from the 'Kensington Posh' of thirty years ago, which tended to be flat and drawling with some affected vowels and diphthongs, used as a signal of class-identity: 'I say you've got a friff'ly nice hice', 'he hed his het on his hyed'. This mode of speech is a valid accent in itself, known as 'advanced R.P.', and is associated with remote upper-class people, especially the elderly: a turn of the century eighty year old Etonian peer might speak in this way. In a growingly egalitarian world it is also a device used by socially pretentious people (see Hyacinth Bucket). The interesting speaker should aim to use as large a range of notes as possible, at least a spoken octave, more for the classics. The object should be to extend the range upward and downward by at least two notes either way, but always from the true 'centre' of your own voice. We all want a deeper, more velvety voice than we actually possess. A consistently deep growling voice is limiting, as is a perpetually shrill voice. The range of the voice also has an effect on the way the actor is cast, since the actor and the role are usually a preconceived idea in someone else's head: the director's head.

The actor's true vocal range can be found out quite simply. Sing, to a doh-ray-me scale the lowest note you can *comfortably* reach, whilst still producing a good tone and volume. Now speak on that note, and sing and speak your way up the scale: about four to six notes above that bottom note is your 'middle note', the note you use most naturally when speaking, and the level round which your voice centres. Continue upward until you reach the highest comfortable note for singing and speaking. Read a few lines of highly dramatic and excited dialogue, and consider how many of those notes you have used. The tape recorder is a useful assistant in exploring the way you're using voice and speech. Some actors and some voice teachers shy away from it, but you can't be self-conscious about objectively testing the first tool of your trade. It must be used calmly and sensibly, as an adjunct to improving acting skill, and you can put yourself in the audience's place. Ask:

1 Is this interesting to listen to?
2 Am I getting stuck in patterns of notes, or repeat inflections?
3 At the top and bottom of my range, does the quality of tone vary, perhaps strident at the top and gruff at the bottom end?

An actor must develop his musical sense, for the note is the musical part of speaking, and without a sense of the tunes of verse or even prose speech, he or she is going to be a dry and unmoving actor, however articulate or intelligent. So the actor should take an acute and intelligent interest in music, especially musical theatre and opera, in how the musical drama, where the note is paramount, makes its effect on the audience's emotions. The music of Mozart, Verdi, Rogers and Hammerstein and Sondheim demonstrates the compelling and seductive qualities of the right voice, saying the right things at the right tempo and the right *pitch*. A play or a screenplay is a huge musical tapestry; even the soaps, which are mainly about the realities we're living in, our street, our cops, our nurses, use beguiling and catchy signature tunes, as in *Coronation Street* and *EastEnders*, and the heights of Hollywood schlock have scores played by vast orchestras to increase every dramatic moment. So, without being singsong or moving the note about unnecessarily, the music, the notes of a text, must be thought of, since many prose plays apparently use a heightened form of language: Wilde, Tennessee Williams and Dylan Thomas's sole play, the beautiful, funny and reverberant *Under Milk Wood*, are examples. Even the superb soap *Hill Street Blues* had its own kind of chamber music, rich, realistic everyday speech rippling along mainly in minor keys. It has deserved its popularity for excellence in every department, but especially for the subtle music of its acting.

Speaking: The Articulation

Spoken English is a wonderful instrument for acting, with a vast vocabulary, and the capacity to express a great range of ideas and emotions. It is a 'front of the mouth' language, spoken with the lips, tongue, palate and teeth, and has few guttural sounds. It also has many variations and dialects, some with an extensive vocabulary of their own, like Geordie and Glaswegian. R.P. is an attempt to give consistency to spoken English by establishing a way of making the sounds so that anyone with normal speech can be understood without losing their individuality. Speech is thought and ideas, and an intelligent and expressive character must be spoken with vocal agility. Drop in to a voice class in any drama school, and you'll find a group of apparently bright people endlessly making silly sounds – popopopo oobooboob awsths ahstths esths ohsths and so on. They are striving for mastery over speech, and its combinations of sounds. Try playing a long part in Shakespeare, Shaw and Stoppard and it is obvious why this command is necessary. Characters with inarticulate or strange or accented speech need even more skill in speaking than the easily articulate: 'Oowa' an unhooth hellow. Ethror' 'nerhy 'hing! I ho hoo haw he hruwwle ho hehing hi' a he hivves he a mou'hool o hahuze!' Camille in Feydeau's masterly farce, *A Flea in Her Ear*. He has no roof to his mouth and loves chatting up ladies. Doctor Finache remedies this little defect with a false palate: Camille's gibberish becomes 'What an uncouth fellow. Extraordinary thing! I go to all the trouble of fetching him and he gives me a mouthful of abuse!' Feydeau is merciless about the misfortunes of life. Throughout the entire play Camille's invaluable prosthesis keeps on getting lost, reducing him once again to verbal scrambled-egg.

We are completely dependent for communication on the ability to make a number of sounds. Articulation is by means of vowels and consonants, the vowels give the flowing musical quality to speech; you breathe out, make a note with the larynx, and give the vowel its particular quality by shaping the mouth in a specific way. Consonants are the sounds made by the tongue, lips and teeth in combination that shape the flow of sound into words, giving it sense; vowels on their own are meaningless except in certain words:

I . . o.a. . . . i. .i .. a .e.i.a. .. e.o.i . . . ui. ; .ou . . i. a . . . . e .. oo. i .. o.e.
.gn.r.nc .. s l.k . . d.l.c.t . . x.t.c fr . . t; t. .ch .t . nd th. bl..m .s g.n

Combine vowels and consonants and you get: 'Ignorance is like a delicate exotic fruit; touch it and the bloom is gone' says Lady Cracknell.

The simple vowels
There are two sorts of simple vowels, those made by the shape of the lips, with no movement of the tongue, which lies relaxed in the mouth, and those which are made with relaxed open lips and movement of the blade of the tongue, which moves toward the roof of the mouth. The diagram overleaf shows the changing lip or tongue positions.

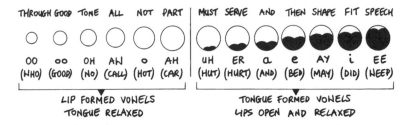

THROUGH GOOD TONE ALL NOT PART | MUST SERVE AND THEN SHAPE FIT SPEECH

| OO | oo | OH | AW | o | AH | UH | ER | a | e | AY | i | EE |
| (WHO) | (GOOD) | (NO) | (CALL) | (HOT) | (CAR) | (HUT) | (HURT) | (AND) | (BED) | (MAY) | (DID) | (WEEP) |

LIP FORMED VOWELS
TONGUE RELAXED

TONGUE FORMED VOWELS
LIPS OPEN AND RELAXED

To form the vowels like this means that they are always consistent. Try the line 'Who do you think you're doing it to?' with the lips in the position for the word car, and it will emerge completely distorted. What is more common is that a vowel is turned into a diphthong (double combination vowels), or that in some dialects a different vowel is used, the Mancunian Booz (as in good) for Bus for example. When studying a regional accent it can be seen that there are a number of differently used vowels which give the dialect its flavour. If we take our line above and for the 'oo' sound substitute the ee-oo diphthong, (see below) we get, 'Heuw deuw yeuw think you're deuwing it teuw?'

The slightest distortion of a simple vowel out of laziness or affectation is sloppy speech: a genuine accent or dialect, where sounds and often words are different from choice, is good speech. A dialect is attractive to listen to, poor and pinched speech tiresome.

Diphthongs

These are double combination vowels where the lips and tongue move their position; some incorporate a transition from tongue to lips, others from lips to tongue. Again, any variation is very noticeable, as we have not seen above:

'Heouw neoew breouwn ceow? (How now brown cow?)' I spent a lot of time during my first term at LAMDA mouthing this immortal phrase, and many others incorporating this sound. Modern theatre and television can make use of the actor with idiosyncratic speech, but he or she will be offered only a limited range of parts. So let's look at the diphthongs, how they are formed, and the common distortions and deformations they're prone to. I'll try to describe them in simple terms.

OY as in joy, boy, annoy: a combination of AW and I, the stress slightly on the first sound, which mustn't be too elongated.

OOER as in poor, dour, tour: of OO as in book and a very short ER, verging on UH. Avoid putting in an intrusive W sound as in power, and avoid pronouncing it as paw, daw, tore.

OW as in house proud: a slightly more, open-mouthed AH to OO as in book. Avoid 'hahse' (Cockney) and 'hice' (Hooray Henry).

AIR as in their fair share: from E as in bed to ER as in hurt. Don't put in an intrusive Y sound, thus: 'theyer fayer shayer', or move the sound toward AH, which would produce something like an advanced R.P. affectation, 'thah thah!'

I as try, sky, high: very short AH sound moving into an I sound as in bit. Frequently altered in speech, for example 'Ay Say!' (the pseudo-genteel) 'Oy don't moynd' (the Liverpudlian) 'Ah trah to bah' (Yorkshire – 'I try to buy').

EE-ER as in fear, near, clear: short I as in hit, moving to ER as in nerve. Avoid the intrusive Y sound as in dee-yer for dear, also fyah, dyah, hyah, which are affected advanced R.P.

The triphthongs

These sounds, like the diphthongs need skilful management.

YOOER as in pure, cure: EE-OO-ER. Avoid pyor, cyor, and pewer.

IER as in fire, mire: a very crisp AH-EE-ER, the final ER bordering on UH. Once again avoid the intrusive Y, fiyer.

OUR as in power, flower, dower: a short AH-EE-ER. This time the intrusive W is lying in waiting: POW-WER. Also the affected 'pahs that be', carrying a 'bunch of flahs'.

Clifford Turner emphasised the irritating common fault of intrusive Y's and W's, most especially when words ending in a vowel are followed by words beginning with a vowel, for example 'so early' not 'so wearly'; 'the evening' not 'the yevening'. It's very easy to fall into this bad habit, and is an example of unclear speech. The actor's special skill is speaking with ultra-clarity, even when playing a character who isn't an educated speaker. Take Alfred Doolittle from Shaw's *Pygmalion*: 'What am I, Governors both? I ask you, what am I? I'm one of the undeserving poor, that's what I am ...' Shaw has cheated a bit by making his dustman an eloquent and impressive natural speaker. So whilst he's a Cockney to his fingertips, unmistakably so, he doesn't speak sloppily, which could sound like this: 'Wo' am I, gu'ners bof? I ar skew, wo' a mi? I mwun uv the yunderserving paw, tha' swo' tiy am...'

Excruciatingly bad speech, and Higgins and Pickering who clearly admire his talent for speaking would not do so if he delivered such vocal slop. The trick of playing Doolittle is to play the vowels ringingly in Cockney (he probably has a wonderful time with POO-ER), but to play the consonants with skill. Doolittle relishes speaking, and is undoubtedly the most entertaining man in his local pub.

The consonants

Consonants give words shape and meaning. Try this little speech with your upper and lower jaws about an inch apart (check with the depth of the middle joint of your thumb): Last night I went out in the cold. It was freezing, but I hoped that if I walked briskly I'd get warm. Then I went home, and retired to bed with a hot water bottle. This is how it will probably sound: Las ni I wen ou' in ner col. I' oo'as hreezing, 'u' I hoked tha' i' I oo'aw 'riskly I' ge' ooarm. Then I ooent ho' 'an retire' ooith a ho' wa'er 'o'le.

It's like trying to dance with your ankles tied together. Misplacing consonants, or making them incorrectly, or making them too softly, will result in woolly speech and lack of sense, however varied the note or beautiful the tone, and one faulty consonant can dominate speech at the expense of sense: Parliament is the wock on which our gweatest twaditions are founded. The mispronounced 'r' has so striking an effect that it overwhelms character, and can be a large part of a characterisation. The sibilant S has the same effect, but is much more irritating to listen to.

Different dramatic material, different acting styles, portraying people of different class and education may need subtle adjustment of the use of the consonants. Most naturalistic acting is everyday speech used in an everyday manner, so the consonants are mainly used neatly and lightly, but there is a difference between a play presented on a stage in a large theatre and the same play being acted for television. The stage is going to need more strength and precision, as well as more voice than the microphone, and big-stage acting sounds mannered and hammy on television or radio. Poetic language of another period of history needs a special technique, because it's what director John Barton (a master of Elizabethan and Jacobean language) calls 'heightened speech' where the explosive consonants are more explosive than in everyday speech, and the R sound is frequently rolled and tapped. Here is Aaron the Moor, from *Titus Andronicus*:

> Now climbeth Tamora Olympus' top,
> Safe out of fortune's shot, and sits aloft
> Secure of thunder's crack or lightning flash,
> Advanced above pale envy's threat'ning reach...

Aaron is a powerful, dangerous man in every department: big, black, clever, sexy, and totally void of pity, morality or conscience. This is the beginning of a soliloquy, and he's thrilled with his good fortune: his mistress has become Empress of Rome. So in speaking it, the actor must capture Aaron's demonic excitement, energy and incisiveness. It's not enough to have a deep and vibrant voice (an asset for Aaron); he must be able to use language and certain sounds need to crack like a whiplash:

> Now Climbeth Tamora Olympus' ToP
> Safe out of Fortune's ShoT, and sits alofT
> Secure of THunder's CRack or lightning's FlaSH
> AdvanceD aBove Pale envy's THreat'ning Reach...

Whilst the vowels and dipthongs may be 'Africanised', the actor must use certain sounds strongly in this speech. I've emphasised certain consonants and consonantal combinations, C, D, P and T especially. 'ToP', 'SHoT', 'alofT' use explosive consonants, which really must be explosive, and F and TH also have an explosive quality: R is 'tapped' twice, that is, the tongue tip hits the hard palate just above the teeth twice, instead of once. It's now beginning to appear that the actor speaking is using a lot of precise and chosen skill, and that the speech of educated or intelligent people is not an adequate instrument for an actor. That anyone can act is a common misunderstanding.

So, let's look at the consonants, how they are made, and which are most important to the actor, apart from R and S, which are the most fallible.

Consonants – Shaping the Words

Basically consonants are of two types: voiced, when the vocal cords vibrate, and the sound has a note and a quality of tone; and unvoiced, that is they consist only of breath, shaped by the mouth, lips or tongue in a particular way. First, voiced, with a following note:

B (boo), D (debt), hard G as in gorge, J as in jam, L as in lead M, N, NG as in singing, R, TH as in them, V, Z, ZH, a soft sound as in leisure. More of these in a minute.

Next, voiceless: they all have something of a hissing quality, which is why they are so difficult for the actor.

CH as in choose, F, H, K or hard C (king, corn), P, SH as in sugar, T.

The explosive consonants
Like the word that's used to describe them, these consonants are an explosion of breath, vital for clarity and energy; breath is contained,

then quickly or suddenly released. They are: B and P. C and G. D and T. I've grouped them in pairs because each sound in the pair is made in a similar way, B and P by compressing and releasing the lips so that the air in the mouth bursts out; C or K and G with the blade of the tongue pressed against the roof of the mouth and then released; D and T, with the pressure chamber formed by pressing the tongue tip against the hard palate just above the top teeth. B(blast) D(doubt) G(good) are voiced, made in the way I've described above. Their unvoiced mates are P(pipe) T(time) C(cage). The difference between B and P is that lip pressure is softer for B than for P, so B is a softer sound. D and T are different because the tongue pressure is gentler for D, and the tongue is taken away more rapidly when forming the T sound: K is a more explosive sound than G. Get used to making the difference between them by using this exercise – first just the sounds ka ga ga ka a dozen or so times, enough to gain a little agility; don't even bother to count, it's not important how many times you do it; then der ter ter der and paw baw baw paw. The tongue and lips at first will be somewhat unresponsive, so practise every day, using a different vowel each time. Start slowly, and increase the speed. Think clearly of what sound you're using, then go for it. Energetic, enthusiastic but untrained actors are often pulled up for 'gabbling', which simply means unclear rushed speech. Pick some words to make the practice more interesting: kick goal, goal kick, day time time day, push back back push etc. These are the actor's five-finger exercises.

The other consonants of an explosive nature are J for jam, ZH in leisure, which is voiced, and CH for church, which is unvoiced. Both are made by pressing the whole of the blade of the tongue against the roof of the mouth, firmly in the case of CH, softer for J.

Pronounce ZH as CH, but the tongue tip only is not pushed against the palate, only the blade. L is not an explosive consonant, although it is made rather like a T by pressing the uplifted tongue tip against the palate just where the top teeth join it. It needs great delicacy but firmness of the tongue-tip, and some people have a 'lazy' tongue, which is not agile or flexible enough to get in exactly the right position. The resultant sound is like this: Wiw you please clean out the wew, and then fiw the gowfish poow? (Will you please clean out the well and fill the goldfish pool?) This is a burden suffered by Cockney speakers, usually caused by sheer sloppiness. The first remedy is to practise trilling the tongue tip, each example in one breath – lalalalalalala, lawlawlawlawlawlaw, etc., using all the simple vowels, then ooloolooloolool, erlerlerlerlerl and so on, putting the L sound in the middle of the word; for some reason this is easier to do. If you make no progress with this sound, or the defective R sound, get the help of a speech therapist.

Nasal consonants: M, N, NG

These are voiced consonants, and have a musical quality because the sound is resonated in the nasal cavity. M is made with the lips, with the blade of the tongue pressed against the hard palate. N is made with the blade and the tip of the tongue against the palate; in this case the sound comes out of the mouth and nostrils at the same time. With NG the blade of the tongue is against the hard palate, further back than M. M and N have a slightly explosive quality, NG has a humming quality, and all three sounds are dependent on nasal resonance. Pinch your nostrils, and try to make the sound. That's why a common cold is such a disaster for the actor or singer. The phrase 'giving no money' is handy for this little test.

The R sound

This sound is voiced, and is one of the most important sounds in dramatic speech, found in several different forms. If it's defective, it influences our whole impression of the speaker. It was a quirk beloved of nineteenth century writers – Dickens' Lord Muttanhead, from *The Pickwick Papers*, speaking of his mail coach and horse: '...painted wed, and with a cweam piebald! Glowious! Glowious!'

Tony Richardson in his film about the charge of the Light Brigade *The Reason Why* had the sillier and more bone-headed of Lord Cardigan's officers all speaking this way, a prodigious affectation known as 'the Coxcomb lisp'.

The R sound is properly made by lifting the very tip of the tongue to the ridges of the hard palate just above the teeth, touching it lightly, and lowering it. The other forms of the sound are the once-tapped, ('terr/rribly' 'sorr/rry' – more emphatic) twice tapped, and rolled R, where the tongue tip taps against or vibrates against the palate. In the case of the rolled R this vibration of the tongue tip is like the brief purring of a cat, not to excess, just about three taps. It's a different sound from the French guttural R, as it's right in the front of the mouth, and the actor must practise hard to master it. It gives muscle to speech, as the explosives do, and is essential for Shakespearian or poetic speech, which is speech at its most powerful.

A common problem with the R sound is its frequent intrusion where it shouldn't be, between two vowels, ending one word and starting another: firan brimstone, loran order. To deal with this hold a *very* tiny pause after the first word, articulating it carefully till you've got it right. It all takes time and work. That is why the finest actors need many weeks of rehearsal, even with their skill and experience.

The S and Z sounds

These consonants are fraught with danger if they're not right; they can both be sibilant, that is hissing or whistling, (again so dominant a speech defect that it needs the attention of the speech therapist) or lisped: 'Tho speakth the thage, for all thy dayth, thy thealouth thlavery ith ended....' This is a bit of nonsense I've made up to demonstrate the devastating effect of a lisp, which is most distressing for the sufferer, again a result of 'lazy tongue'. This problem also needs speech therapy, and its correction is a huge liberation for the person concerned; to suffer from a problem in speaking is to be subject to constant misunderstanding and sometimes ridicule. Two eminent British politicians of the last twenty years were mercilessly sent up, because one said 'My honowable fwiend' and the other 'Neouw I hope this heouse will ceount itself lucky...'. They shall be nameless – both men of distinction. Good speech isn't so important for a politico as it is for an actor!

The sibilants are a problem for the actor and need a perfect relationship between the tongue tip and the upper teeth: if the tongue tip is too bulky or inflexible the result will be a lisp, a hiss, or saliva delivered into the orchestra pit. Politicians again: *Spitting Image* was very unkind about a certain politician with a problem S, and represented him as an oratorical lawn-sprinkler every time he opened his mouth; having a sense of humour, he's taken it in good part.

S an Z are unvoiced, and made by lifting the tongue forward, very close behind the upper front teeth for S, slightly lower and more relaxed for Z. This is fine in theory, but the shape and position of the teeth can produce a hiss or a whistle, which can reach the back of the largest theatres, blotting out other sounds and driving the audience mad. I remember the actor Edward Atienza playing an ancient ga-ga Archbishop in a high voice and with a piercing whistle; it was very funny, you waited for the next whistle to ambush him. And it didn't matter that you couldn't understand what he said, as he talked nonsense anyway. The point is, he was a very old man, a sacred person, quite dotty, and having trouble with his dentures – a banana-skin waiting for every great man. The first step to remedy this problem is to practise withdrawing the tongue sooner, and exercising the tongue tip in conjunction with the upper teeth. You may need dentistry to correct the size, shape and position of the teeth, but it's better to overcome the problem by working on the tongue. In the next chapter I'll suggest some exercises for greater tongue flexibility.

The TH sounds

These are TH as in think and TH as in them. They are made with the tongue tip touching the bottom edge of the upper teeth, and then withdrawing it, releasing the breath and note. TH(ink) has a lightly explosive quality; TH(em) has a gentler quality, and the tongue tip is lowered more slowly. A problem with the first TH sound is when it follows F, as in baths, fifths, etc., which can emerge as barfs and fiffs.

F and V sounds

F and V, are the reverse of the TH sounds, made by the conjunction of the lower edge of the front upper teeth with the lower lip. As with all the paired consonants, the difference is one of pressure: there is a rapid dropping of the lower lip for F, a gentler one for V. F as in fox again has a slightly explosive quality. In rare cases V is substituted for F, mainly by actors playing southern English country yokels on children's television programmes: We veels the vorce of them gales down on the varm!

This has been a summary of the basic tools of voice and speech. The student of acting who means business must go deeply into how he uses both: it's much more complex than it first appears, and applies equally to those who have been brought up with standard southern English speech, received pronunciation. Probably more than ninety percent of contemporary professional actors have been trained, and a trained voice and skill with R.P. is the starting point for all roles.

In the next chapter we'll look at the voice and speech in action, but meanwhile here are a few vocal exercises for you to work on.

Relaxation for the whole body

1 Start by using the relaxation exercises described in Chapter 2.

2 Stand with the feet slightly apart. Raise the arms and stretch upward; look upward, reach for the sky. Now let the arms slowly fall, from wrists to shoulders, as the head falls on to the chest. Let the spine melt from the top, at the same time as letting the knees bend, so that your whole body is making a shape like a letter S, and slowly and gently crumple down to the floor.

3 Roll on to your back, legs and arms spread out. Breathe in deeply and easily, lowering the diaphragm. Breathe out, first from the diaphragm, getting some help from gravity as the solar plexus sinks in. Continue breathing like this for a minute or so

4 Now tighten and release all the muscles in order. Try to use separate sets of muscles without involving others, as if you were picking up a

pencil with your toes, but not the leg, body, torso, arms and face. The tense actor is usually tense overall. So imagine yourself floating, and tighten and clench the feet; hold for a few seconds whilst checking that this doesn't involve the whole leg, then waggle the feet and release the tension.

5 Proceed up the body, calves, thighs, buttocks, stomach muscles, in each case tightening, holding and releasing, whilst continuing to breath easily. Don't overbreathe, try to establish a smooth and easy rhythm. Now to the chest, shoulders, arms and hands. In each case see how much other parts of the body are involved; can you clench your fist without involving your shoulder? Now the shoulders and neck. Are you grimacing, gritting your teeth? Lastly, the face; tighten and release all the facial muscles several times. Check that breathing is smooth and rhythmic. Stand up, easily.

Exercises for the jaw, lips and tongue
1 Waggle the jaw only, from side to side, up and down, forward and backward till the jaw moves easily – don't jerk it. Stretch the lips wide, then purse them. Push them up as far as possible, then down. Repeat this many times, to make them as flexible as possible.

2 Stick out your tongue then withdraw it, repeating this often. Now protrude the tongue as far as possible and rotate it in both directions. Try to touch the tip of your nose with the tip of your tongue, then the point of the chin. With the lips wide open, protrude the tongue, and bring up the sides, making it into a tube. Repeat all these for a few minutes until the tongue aches, which it should.

3 Now with the jaw in a comfortable open position, lightly and firmly touch the hard palate just above the upper teeth and the back of the lower teeth, using only the tongue tip, changing from upper to lower as rapidly as possible.

In all these exercises to improve the articulation try not to let tensions creep into face, neck or any part of the body. Their object is to turn breath, voice and speech into an instrument which responds to the actor's thoughts and instincts.

An exercise for tone
This exercise is for sustaining tone, to keep the resonant quality of the voice constant during movement of the voice, from vowel to vowel, note to note, loud to soft. Be patient and make sure you grasp the sequence before doing the exercise. It's like knowing the lines.

You can't give a performance, convey meanings or make sense unless the text is securely known.

Start on your lowest comfortable note, and ascending note by note speak and sing each pair of sounds, both loudly and softly: Hah Hoo Hah Hee Hah Hoo Hah Hee as many times as necessary, over as many notes as you can. Try the sequence very softly, and repeat it getting gradually louder. OO to EE through AH represent the extreme ends of the vowel scale. You're trying to coax the voice into action, and stretch the range of notes whilst sustaining tone. At the top and bottom of your note range, and at either end of the volume range, the sound may go harsh or husky, so make these sounds gently. Don't force your voice. Make a series of combinations using any of the simple vowels, Haw Her Hay, Hee Hu Ho. It's a kind of incantation where you make a habit of finding the sound, finding the volume, finding the tone without having to think about it. If you find it too complicated, deal with only one element at a time such as getting the vowel right, or increasing volume, or changing the note. Note that each sound is preceded by the aspirate H, to make attack easier. When you're at home with the exercise, place your hands on the ribs and solar plexus to see how the breathing is working: that H will make pushing out the sound with the diaphragm easier.

An exercise for resonance

Sing or intone, then speak Mah Nah Ngah Moo Noo Ngoo May Nay Ngay Mee Nee Ngee. Use all the other vowel sounds with these nasal consonants. The object is to avoid sounding nasal, yet make use of the nasal cavities as resonators; the tonal quality must not change when you use nasal consonants. Go through the sounds in reverse, i.e. Ahm Ahn Ahng, etc.

Practice with consonants

Deal with the explosives first. PahBah BahPah PahBah BahPah PahBah, KooGoo GooKoo KooGoo GooKoo, DayTay TayDay DayTay TayDay and so on. Do this all quite a few times, varying the pace, and aim to make each one a perfect crisp explosion. A few tongue twisters:

> Round the rugged rocks the ragged rascal ran.
> Peter Piper picked a peck of pickled peppers.
> Frenzied fleas fly frantically forward.
> Quick quotes quell querulous questions.
> The Leith police dismisseth us.
> Peggy Babcock Peggy Babcock Peggy Babcock Peggy Babcock...

Next, some of those ghastly consonantal combinations: they do happen in actual speech, not often thank goodness, but you don't want to shower your fellow actors with spray, spit your false teeth half-way across the stage, or any of the other comic speech disasters that befall actors:

> Oost Ohst Awst Ahst Ayst Eest. Oozd Ohzd Awzd Ayzd
> Eezd. Ookt Ohkt Awkt etc. Ooskt Oskt Awskt etc. Oosths
> Ohsths Awsths etc. Oofths Ohfths Awfths etc. Oontl Ohntl
> Awntl etc. Oobl Ohbl Awbl...

Make sure that you practise all the simple vowels with these consonantal combinations. These are examples of the exercises that the actor must practise during his training, and after. It needs a lot of willpower to practise in solitude, so use the tape-recorder for feedback, or better still, work with a few like-minded friends.

4
Speaking the Text: Voice in Action

We've examined the principal tool of the actors' trade, voice and speech, looking at what you need, and the beginnings of how to develop vocal skills. Now let's look at how you use them. All the work of rehearsal, digging and examining, researching and discussing, discovering character, relationships, objectives, the way the dramatist has chosen to present character and situation (the *style* of the play) must finally be realised in performance, where the characters tell the story, and live the experiences. The play must be brought to life by speech, and at every performance the text must be spoken as if it had never been said before; to the audience it's happening now, on the stage, on the screen. However, the apparent spontaneity of what's happening, what's being said, is the product of the actors' artifice. The actors have dug deeply to find every possible meaning that the play contains. With help from the director they have decided what they're saying: descriptions, statements, narratives, subtle intimations, heartfelt declarations, lies, evasions, exaggerations, rhetoric, bullshit, ordinary human interchanges. The actor must now find out how the use of language and speech can convey all of these meanings in a multitude of situations, and how he or she must employ speech to keep the audience's attention and interest.

Inflection

Spoken English is an inflected language, that is, we convey our meaning not just by the words we use but by the way we modify and bend spoken words. There are a number of ways of doing this, the most important of which are change of note, variations of speed and rhythm, fluctuations between loud and soft, and the use of pause and silence. This is known as inflection. All dramatic dialogue has to develop a shape, of high and low, fast and slow, loud and soft, all these variations serving one purpose: conveying meaning. Just living and talking to people, getting on with life and work has taught

51

us all that skill, but it's not enough for the actor who is packing into his performance an intensity of experience lasting two hours or more – human existence condensed. In a very short time we take the audience through years of life, round the world, into the past. Sometimes the purpose and meaning of a life is explained, its success or failure; or the drama may present a picture of a particular place, at a particular time.

All variations in speech emerge from the need to find the right way of conveying meaning. Yet even experienced and talented actors need notes from the director to help them to find the most effective way of finding expression and giving vocal 'shape' to their acting. Here are some of the things that happen in individual performances. Probably the most frequently given note by directors is 'keep up the inflection'. A rising note at the end of a phrase or line or sentence is a signal to keep on listening:

> The last time she was in a church was when she was married to me. I expect that surprises you, doesn't it? It was expediency, pure and simple. We were in a hurry, you see. Yes, we were actually in a hurry! Lusting for the slaughter! Well, the local registrar was a particular pal of Daddy's, and we knew he'd spill the beans to the Colonel like a shot. So we had to seek out some local vicar who didn't know him quite so well. But it was no use. When my best man – a chap I'd met in the pub that morning – and I turned up, Mummy and Daddy were in the church already. They'd found out at the last moment, and had come to watch the execution carried out. How I remember looking down at them, full of beer for breakfast, and feeling a bit buzzed. Mummy was slumped over her pew in a heap – the noble, female rhino, pole-axed at last! And Daddy sat beside her, upright and unafraid, dreaming of his days among the Indian Princes, and unable to believe he'd left his horsewhip at home. Just the two of them in that empty church – them and me. (*Coming out of his remembrance suddenly.*) I'm not sure what happened after that. We must have been married, I suppose. I think I remember being sick in the vestry.
> (*To Alison.*) Was I?
>
> (Jimmy Porter, *Look Back in Anger* by John Osborne)

You may have captured Jimmy's anguish and fury, his sense of mockery, his sarcastic cruelty, but that's not going to guarantee that the speech will hold the audience's interest. Jimmy is a burnt child, his intelligence, education and abilities wasted in the world he finds himself in. He's negative and destructive, and doesn't know how to help himself or anyone else. Yet this speech is full of wry humour, and fizzes with energy; it's an account of a mortifying fiasco, absolutely

Kenneth Haigh, Helena Hughes and Mary Ure in the historic first production of **Look Back in Anger.**

honest, and he doesn't spare himself. Note that it's written in very short sentences, nineteen of them in a speech of two dozen lines. A question mark does indicate a rising inflection but full stops imply pause, 'let them take in what I've just said'. Try reading the first ten lines letting the note of the voice drop as you come to each fullstop; it will produce a series of curt gloomy statements, with the added problem that you will repeat the same pattern of notes, and give the speech funereal slowness. So Jimmy becomes a morose and crashing bore instead of a man we feel for and listen to, in spite of his catastrophic behaviour and childish belief that there's no good in any

53

one. Jimmy is something of an actor (Osborne was an actor), and makes a good story of it, *purely by the way he tells it*; otherwise it's unforgivable, an unnecessary anecdote calculated to humiliate his wife Alison and mock his guest, the cool actress Helena.

So we must find a way of playing it that makes it interesting to listen to, despite its awful burden of cruel and insulting ridicule. First, a crisp and cracking pace, but not rushed; he uses the full stops as pauses to see that his barbs have gone home.

> The last time she was in a church was when she was married to me. (*A pause of a couple of beats, whilst he looks from Alison to Helena.*) I expect that surprises you, doesn't it? (*A rising inflection, said with light sarcasm. Another short pause, keeping his eyes on Helena.*) It was expediency, pure and simple. (*Two ways of doing this line – he might stress the words 'pure and simple' sarcastically, with a level inflection, or just say them lightly and ironically.*) We were in a hurry, you see. (*Osborne's stage direction is 'The comedy of this strikes him at once, and he laughs'.*) Yes, we were actually in a hurry! (*Probably a rising inflection on 'hurry' as he turns to look at Alison, who is paralysed with shame and embarrassment.*) Lusting for the slaughter! (*a beat, then briskly.*) Well, the local registrar was a particular pal of Daddy's, and we knew he'd spill the beans to the Colonel like a shot. So we had to seek out some local vicar who didn't know him quite so well. (*This passage is the story racing on, so to give it continuity – 'pal of Daddy's', 'like a shot', and 'quite so well' are all probably played on a rising note – 'quite so well' can be strongly ironic.*) But it was no use.

'But it was no use' is a tag-line to the first part of the story, and probably played for melodrama, the first real falling inflection so far in the speech. This isn't a blueprint for how to play the speech, or how to play Jimmy; different actors will give emphasis to different aspects of his personality. But there can be no doubt that the speech, like all dramatic speech, has to be taken apart and reassembled with a particular quality of inflection, timing and a sense of comedy (Jimmy dramatises and exaggerates). So the rising inflection sustains speech and gives continuity to thought; the falling inflection makes the audience think for a moment about what's just been said.

There is a school of thought, much influenced by a misinterpretation of Stanislavsky and more popular in America, which believes that if you get the intentions of a character right (often called 'motivation') and you have researched profoundly into experiences and circumstances which parallel those your character undergoes, the lines and meanings will largely take care of themselves. This will only happen in the case of very talented and experienced actors. The speaking of text has to be worked on, and 'spontaneity' is not created by feeling it and hoping it comes out OK. With half his mind the actor must think 'somebody is telling me these things, do I understand their obvious meaning, and their hidden meanings?'

Interplay in Dialogue

When two or more actors are speaking in a scene, they must listen acutely to what the other is saying. Not only is the actor saying the lines as if they'd never been said before, the hearers are apparently hearing them for the first time. And if each actor identifies with the character and feels emotion about his situation, the dialogue is going to be different almost every time. Actors working together are in effect making a construction of speech which is capable of subtle change, but is basically a well put together piece of machinery. It is equally important that each actor is conscious of his or her character within the play as a whole; they must not only know why *they* are having that conversation, they must know why the *other* person is having it. A big hazard in dialogue is the fault known as 'picking up each other's tone', which is a misnomer for picking up each other's inflection, tonal pattern and perhaps tempo as well. Imagine a play cast with actors who all sounded alike, all baritones, all sopranos, all using the same tempo, and all dropping their voices at the end of the lines. It could only be made worse if they all looked identical. So actors speaking together are doing something which requires the utmost mutual under-standing, and the greatest skill and finesse in passing the thoughts and feelings of the characters to and fro. A very good example of bad acting is when actors are not listening and reacting, but merely waiting for their turn to speak, which makes for a series of isolated utterances.

Here's a piece of dialogue full of variety of inflection and tempo, from *The Caretaker* by Harold Pinter. The mysterious and possibly dangerous Mick has discovered a tramp, Davies (a Welshman) sleeping in his house:

MICK	Did you sleep here last night?
DAVIES	Yes.
MICK	Sleep well?
DAVIES	Yes.
MICK	Did you have to get up in the night?
DAVIES	No.
	(*A pause*)
MICK	What's your name?

TO21918

DAVIES	(*shifting, about to rise*) Now, look here...
MICK	What?
DAVIES	Jenkins.
MICK	Jen-kins.
	(*Davies makes a sudden movement to rise. A violent bellow from Mick sends him back.*)
MICK	(*shouts*) Sleep here last night?
DAVIES	Yes.
MICK	(*continuing at great pace*) How'd you sleep?
DAVIES	I slept ...
MICK	Sleep well?
DAVIES	Now, look ...
MICK	What bed?
DAVIES	That ...
MICK	Not the other?
DAVIES	No!
MICK	Choosy. (*He pauses. Quietly*) Choosy. (*He pauses. Amiably*) What sort of sleep did you have in that bed?
DAVIES	(*banging the floor*) All right!
MICK	You weren't uncomfortable?
DAVIES	(*groaning*) All right.
	(*Mick rises and stands over Davies*)
MICK	You a foreigner?
DAVIES	No.
MICK	Born and bred in the British Isles?
DAVIES	I was.
MICK	What did they teach you? (*He pauses, moves to the bed and looks at it*) How did you like my bed? (*He pauses*) That's my bed. You want to mind you don't catch a draught.
	(*Davies stares warily at Mick, who turns. Davies rises, scrambles to the clothes-horse and seizes his trousers. Mick moves swiftly and grabs the trousers from Davies who lunges for them. Mick holds out a hand warningly.*)
	You intending to settle down here?
DAVIES	Give me my trousers, then.
MICK	You settling down for a long stay?
DAVIES	Give me my bloody trousers!
MICK	Why, where are you going?
DAVIES	Give me and I'm going. I'm going to Sidcup.

This passage presents the problem of how to convey the most meaning with the smallest amount of dialogue. Pinter never pads, never wastes a word. Yet he never provides a mass of likely information about who his characters are, and when they speak about themselves it's fascinating, but possibly untrue; an odd mixture of reminiscence, peripheral and often useless information. Mick, again:

> You know, believe it or not, you've got a funny kind of resemblance to a bloke I once knew in Shoreditch. Actually he lived in Aldgate. I was staying with a cousin in Camden Town. This chap, he used to have a pitch in Finsbury Park, just by the bus depot...

So we have a writer who writes dialogue which is often Spartan, pregnant with meaning below the banal surface, and long speeches like great cocoons spun out of the subconscious, the half-remembered.

Back to the scene; how might it be played? First, it's a meeting between two aggressive men. Next, they discuss at length whether or not Davies slept in what Mick says is his bed, and how he slept; then, who Davies is, and what his future intentions are. 'Pinteresque' is now a description of a way of speaking and behaving and a kind of atmosphere full of implicit menace, the more uneasy for not being explained. There's a lot going on below the surface: Mick's threatening, probing and assertion of power, shifty evasions and growing fear from Davies. The dialogue consists of seventeen words of two or more syllables, and one hundred and nineteen monosyllables. It looks at first like a chat between two extremely inarticulate men, but this is disproved by the fact that at other times they are very eloquent about misty attitudes which largely exist in their own heads. They are both liars. Real feelings are hidden: Mick's seemingly friendly enquiry 'sleep well?' is only a false civility, and his ferocity and anger might be more apparent than real. Davies is almost entirely monosyllabic, a man as close as a clam, who's been in many a dodgy situation, and has learned to button his lip. Yet each 'yes' and 'no' has an exact meaning and mood. Repetition of words, simple and complicated, has one rule: find a way of saying the same word with a number of different meanings, a different emphasis, a different inflection. Let's look at the scene again:

MICK	(chattily, lightly) Did you sleep here last night?
DAVIES	(A pause, slowly, trying to read Mick's enigmatic face) Ye...es.
MICK	(Pleasantly) Sleep well?
DAVIES	(Surprised and wary, but more openly) Yes. (It's almost a question, 'what the hell are you asking me for?')
MICK	(Almost with a wink of complicity, as if to say, have you been pissing in my saucepans?) Did you have to get up in the night?

DAVIES	(With a vigorous shake of the head) NO! (meaning not me, I'm not one of those dirty slags!)
	A pause. Mick, with a little grin, looks Davies up and down. Davies, uncomfortable, looks sideways, not down.
MICK	(Harder, quicker, a little louder) What's your name?
DAVIES	(He starts. Opens and shuts his mouth a couple of times) NOW, look here... (Mick takes a step towards him, the smile is tight.)
MICK	(As if he'd misheard) What? (He fires it at him)
DAVIES	(Thrown) Ah ... uh ... Jenkins.
MICK	(Smiles indulgently, nods slowly a couple of times) Jenkins. (possibly implying, you stupid old prat, if you were English you'd say your name was Smith or Brown.)
MICK	(Bellows fiercely) SLEEP HERE LAST NIGHT?
DAVIES	(Terrified, hastily.) YES!
MICK	(Crowding him, rather fiercely, with a horrible grin) HOW'D YOU SLEEP?
DAVIES	(Stammering) I-I-slept...
MICK	(Making it sound as though there was some terrifying reason why Davies' sleep should have been disturbed.) SLEEP WELL? (On a rising inflection)
DAVIES	(Trying to reply quickly, but mouthing; trying to assert himself) Now, LOOK! ... (He runs out of words)
MICK	(After a pause, he looks hard at Davies, then, flatly and precisely) What ... bed?
DAVIES	(Wildly; he casts his eyes about before he finds the bed) That ...
MICK	(Rapidly, cutting in) Not the other?
DAVIES	(A wail of fear and exasperation) Nooo!
	(A momentary pause. Davies swivels his eyes round to peek at Mick. Mick gives a little whistle, nods again and says:)
MICK	Choosy. (Choooo-sy! almost implying that Davies is a man of taste and discernment.) *Choosy.*
	(Amiably, too amiably, as if discussing the Ritz)
	What sort of sleep did you have in that bed?
DAVIES	(Desperate at being played with, losing his rag) ALL RIGHT!
MICK	(Solicitously) You weren't ... uncomfortable?
DAVIES	(Beaten, shaking his head slowly from side to side – in a small voice) All right ...
	Mick rises and stands over Davies.
MICK	(Coldly, condescendingly) You ... a foreigner? (deliberately laden with hatred and prejudice)
	And so on.

*Peter Firth and Donald Pleasance as Mick and Davies in **The Caretaker***

Mick picks words and fires them like bullets. In examining this scene you can see that it's almost impossible to separate speaking from all the other things that are happening; who is looking at whom, bodily demeanour, what the characters are feeling and understanding, moves, the general atmosphere. What Pinter brought sharply to our attention is that drama doesn't need pages of plausible explanation about how the characters got to this point, who they are, what the situation is, exactly where it's happening, why it's happening. Whilst the actor must satisfy himself that he's got enough background knowledge to be able to understand character and scene, it should be known facts, agreed by the actor and director, derived from the text. How clean is Davies likely to be? How healthy? If you gave him a shave and a haircut and put him in smart clothes, what would he look like? What was his last meal? Probably someone's discarded fish and chips, hauled out of a litter bin. Particularly, where in Wales does he come from, how much education has he had? These two will determine his accent and mode of speech. He's a most particular Welshman, not just a token figure of a poor Welshman, or worse still, a mere joke Taffy. The play needs extremely careful attention to the dialogue the more so because Pinter's characters exist because they say they do. What we see them to be is what they themselves say they are. Mick, like most of Pinter's people, is a man without a past. From the streetwise slang he uses he's probably an intelligent sharp Cockney thug who keeps some very dubious company, but he has a taste for the high falutin', for professional jargon:

> Here he is making an offer to rent to Davies his run-down slum of a house. (Rapidly) Three hundred and fifty a year exclusive. No argument. I mean, if that sort of money's in your range don't be afraid to say so. Here you are. Furniture and fittings, I'll take four hundred or the nearest offer. Rateable value ninety quid for the annum... Say the word and I'll have my solicitors draft you out a contract...

This is cant. Mick is a con-artist, and talking is his living; he can cope with most situations by sensing the way language is used to describe and manipulate them. He can also bully and coerce by an appearance of power and knowledge. His accent is probably slightly London, overlaid with a middle-class accent – an ambiguous combination, and both we and Davies never get to the bottom of him. Yet he seems a very likely sort of bloke. Walk half a mile from street corner to street corner, and you'll find him.

The strongest effect the actor makes is by speaking and conveying his meaning: the sense, the feeling, the time, the place. The dramatist aims to develop character, to let his people reveal themselves. A good play is not always a straightforward narrative of events, but a chiaroscuro study of its characters in motion, meeting opposition and difficulties as they seek to achieve what they really want. To this end they talk just as people do in everyday life. They tell the truth, they tell lies; they tell half-truths, they tell white lies; they own up to what they are, they kid themselves about their true nature. Some people are open and direct, others pretend to be someone they're not, and act phoney, speak phoney, and do phoney things. What is known as 'Comedy of Manners' is usually associated with plays of a past age. The Restoration comedies and the plays of Wilde and Coward are typical examples: stylish comedies, witty, light and swarming with polished elegant people. What really matters is an accurate picture of those characters, their behaviour, values, pleasures and objects of scorn and derision. They are reacting to the values of their age, which constantly change, from a devout and religious society to a warlike one, from an age of great discovery to an age of flippancy and hedonism, from an age of superstition to an age of spiritual or intellectual enlightenment. Hamlet's advice 'to hold the mirror up to nature' still applies.

More Modern Dialogue

Let's look at another scene, and try to find out how the actors actually play it and speak it. The play is *Abigail's Party*, a wickedly astute comedy about suburban values and morals, about how much we react to the injunctions showered on us by the 'Manipulators': the cheaper end of the press, trashy magazines, abominable television commercials, the purveyors of 'taste' and 'style'. Are we actually living, or are we puppets jumping about to the hornpipe of fashion? The play came about in a remarkable way, under the guidance of Mike Leigh; it was the result of the cast's improvisations round a chosen theme emerging from their research and observation of getters and spenders, how they live, what they live in, what they do, how they speak and dress. The people in the play are a product of the 1970s, the upwardly mobile: The children of working-class people, with spending power and education, who want a slice of the good things of life, or what some of them think are the good things. Beverly, the central character, is an attractive woman probably in her early thirties, by profession a 'beautician', that is she sells upmarket make-up in big stores. Her husband Laurence is an estate agent, her guests and new neighbours Angela and Tony are respectively a nurse and a computer operator. Her other neighbour in the play is Susan, who is middle-class, older, divorced and struggling. Beverly is giving 'drinks', to meet her new neighbours, and to show off her house, her furnishings, her clothes. She thinks she's *arrived*.

The heart of the play is the dialogue. It's a series of inane and trivial conversations, led by Beverly, about the only things she knows about, clothes, make-up, houses, furnishings and in an oblique way, sex. Her conversation is peppered with clichés: 'you know what I mean –' 'casting a beady eye on the goings-on', (where she manages two in quick succession.) The W.C. is 'the toilet', her brother has 'a fantastic job', a 'fabulous house' and he gets 'great wages'. She says 'yeah' for 'yes' and 'gonna' for 'going to'. She appears to have learned to speak from watching television soaps and commercials, and to read from Mills and Boon stories. A sample:

BEVERLY   Ang – would you mind if I asked you a personal question?

ANGELA   No.

BEVERLY   Now, please don't be offended when I say this, but, what colour lipstick are you wearing?

ANGELA   A pinky red.

BEVERLY   A pinky red! Now, can you take a little bit of criticism? Please don't be offended when I say this, but, you're wearing a very pretty dress, if I may say so; now, you see that pink ribbon down the front? If you'd chosen, Ang, a colour slightly nearer that pink, I think it would have blended more with your skin tones; d'you know what I mean?

ANGELA   A paler colour.

BEVERLY   A slightly paler colour. Now, can I give you a tip?

ANGELA   (*after a brief pause*) Yes.

BEVERLY   Now, okay. I can see what you've done: you've just sat down in front of your mirror, and you've put your lipstick on. Now, this is something I always used to tell my customers, and it always works. Now, next time, just sit down in front of your mirror, and relax. And just say to yourself, 'I've got very beautiful lips'. Then take your lipstick and apply it, and you'll see the difference, Ang. Because then you will be applying your lipstick to every single corner of your mouth, d'you know what I mean? Will you try it for me next time?

ANGELA   Yes.

BEVERLY   Just sit down in front of your mirror and relax, and say to yourself...

ANGELA   'I've got very beautiful lips.'

BEVERLY   And I promise you'll see the difference, Ang! Okay?

ANGELA   Thanks.

Beverly would appear to be an intolerable fatuous idiot; she is, but in fact she's also very interesting and without realising it, very funny. She is an extraordinary personality, who carries several kinds of

Alison Steadman and Janine Duvitski in **Abigail's Party**

pretentiousness to their extreme limit. She fancies herself as a talker and conversationalist; she's done well, from probably humble beginnings and an appalling education. She's garrulous, brainless and a show-off, who judges only by appearances, and cares nothing for other people. Later in the play, her husband Laurence has a heart-attack – her first reaction is annoyance with him for spoiling her soirée. She's also very attractive and sexy looking. We wait with agonised delight for her next banality, uttered with either passionate belief or a play-acting self-congratulatory smirk. Her accent and mode of speech is what John Mortimer, himself a fine dramatist and master of language, once described as 'Ruislip Mandarin', a combination of preciousness, vulgarity and ornate long-windedness. The accent must match the language. She tries to talk posh, but has a tin ear, and can't do it, and is sublimely unaware of the effect she actually makes. Angela is in some respects from the same stable, but has several redeeming qualities: she has a useful and worthwhile job, cares about the kids she nurses, and is a hopelessly innocent giggler. She's younger than Beverly, easily influenced, but she won't become another Beverly.

Let's try to take the scene apart; again we have to consider all that's going on at the same time as speech.

BEVERLY   Ainge, would you mind if I asked you a ... personal quais-
tion? (Her accent is probably 'Croynge' (a combination of
Croydon and Penge) that is, vaguely south London. She
puts the question with genteel delicacy, as if asking her
what brand of tampons she uses.)

ANGELA   Neu..ow. (I won't go on trying to illustrate their subtly
excruciating vowel sounds, each actress must go out and
listen, and choose for herself.)

BEVERLY   Now, please don't be offended when I say this, but what
colour lipstick are you wearing? (Beverly uses too many
words – 'when I say this' is unnecessary, 'wearing' is a
genteel-ism for 'got on'.)

ANGELA   A pinky red.

BEVERLY   A pinky raid! (Said with a long upward swoop, then
changing, then rattling on solicitously; we must recognise that what she says is sales patter.) Pu-leese don't be
offended wain I sayee this, but, you're wearing a very
pretty draiss, if I may say so; now you see that pink
ribbon down the front? if you'd chosen, Ang, a colour
slightly nearer that pink, it would have blended more
with your skin tones; d'you know what I mean? (Note
how she hijacks Angela's name, turning her into 'Ang',
(Ange) and insists on repeating it.) Her self-importance
makes her pause often, and she monopolises the conversation. She's a bully, disguising it as care and interest.
'Jew no wha'timean' comes out again and again, as a
rising squeak – it's a reflex action, not a question.

ANGELA   A paler colour. (Slightly dimly, after a tiny pause.)

BEVERLY   (Nit picking) A *slightly* paler colour. Now can I give you a
tip? (Ruislip Mandarin cliché again).

ANGELA   (After a brief pause) Yes. (Perhaps she has a feeling that
Beverly's advice will be faintly denigratory.)

BEVERLY   (Launches on the full snake-oil commercial, alternately
mum-ish and breathily seductive) Now, okay (busily) I can
see what you've done: you've just sat down in front of your
mirror and *put your lipstick on.* (Angela looks bewildered;
as a nurse, make-up is a slapdash business, yet for all that
she's an attractive girl. Beverly now moves into her TV
commercial voice, breathily important, low and confid-
ing.) Now, this is something I always used to tell my
customers (tiny pause) and it *always* works. Now (beat)
next time (beat) just sit in front of your mirror, and
relaaax. And just say to yourself (in an arch, dreamy

voice, turning her head to one side) 'I've got (slowly, breathily) ... very ... beautiful ... lips.' (Brightly, up-beat) Then take your lipstick, and *apply* it (another posh cant euphemism for 'put it on') and (with great conviction) you'll see the *difference*, Ang. (Stronger) Because then you will be applying your lipstick to every *single* corner of your mouth. D'you know what I mean? (With sisterly concern) Will you try it for me next time?

ANGELA   ...(Blinking) Yaiss. (She looks round, and breaks into a nervous smile, and giggles.)

BEVERLY   (Like a hypnotist) Just sit down in front of your mirror and relax, and say to yourself...

ANGELA   (Trying to imitate Beverly, but she hasn't Beverly's total conviction; so speaks like a zombie:) 'I've ... got ... very ... beautiful ... lips.' (She has another giggle, and wriggles self-consciously. As she's wearing a very short skirt, we see a lot of leg, which embarrasses her even more.)

BEVERLY   (Like the fairy godmother) And I *promise* you'll see the difference, Ang! OKAY?

ANGELA   (Running her tongue over her lips, then:) Thanks. (She feels out the new, super-kissable mouth. Her husband Tony looks on, a faint resurgence of lust conquering the effect of the beer he's been drinking.)

I've deliberately over-emphasised some of the effects and sounds in Beverly's excruciating accent, which finally needs to be a very subtle set of vocal contortions, as with the other characters. Laurence probably speaks near R.P., but one or two sounds let him down, and he doesn't have that iron command of speech and idiom bred in an English public school, that is, an expensive private school. Tony has probably had a fairly sophisticated technical education, wears good if slightly flash clothes, but he is vocally a surly monosyllabic wally. Angela speaks better and more sensibly than Beverly, but it's still a suburban south-eastern accent. Susan probably has been to a public school, a minor one, and is middle-class through and through; her husband is David, not Dave, and her daughter is Abigail. So we have a profound social comedy of the importance of little differences in What You Say, and How You Say It. All the implied hard work in the previous chapter about mastering vowels, diphthongs and consonants is necessary if the actors are to make this deadly accurate dialogue work; simply understanding and recognising the characters doesn't actually realise them in linguistic terms, but vocal skill and delicacy does. All 'accents' are a variation or departure from R.P., if

R.P. is the simplest and clearest mechanism for spoken English. Some actors who possess a 'good ear' have a great facility for imitating accents, others will have to do it sound by sound, and in the professional theatre, television and films there are plenty of actors available who speak an accent authentically. Not Beverly's, I hasten to add.

Conversation from a Modern Classic

I'm going to look at acting and speaking the language and verse of an earlier century in another chapter, but right now I want us to look at a scene of furious emotion, a violent quarrel, from a great play by a master of 'naturalism'. *The Seagull* is the first of Chekhov's four great masterpieces, first acted in 1896. This version is in most accessible modern English, translated and recreated by Michael Frayn, another master of language and an important contemporary playwright. Chekhov's métier is LIFE. As it really is. He is a serious but comic dramatist who examines the lives of the educated upper middle classes in a Russia heading toward revolution. They are completely at home with European culture, and have time, leisure and the articulateness to examine their feelings, hopes, tastes, passions and philosophies. The major theme of *The Seagull* is about being a creative artist, possessing and developing talent, struggling and suffering for it, effortlessly using it, being disillusioned by your own art, having faith in it. The central characters of the play are two mature artists, both glamorous middle-aged people, both very successful. They are Arkadina, an actress and an undoubted star and her lover Trigorin, a popular and successful novelist. The other two main characters are young, and want to be artists. Konstantin is Arkadina's twenty-five year old son, who wants to be a playwright, and to change and advance the drama; he is in love with Nina, who wants to be an actress. The relationship between Konstantin and his mother swings between extremes of doting love and near hate; she has both spoiled and neglected him. The result is a dreaming, doting, unworldly young man, fighting it out with a mother who is a charming monster of egotism. Arkadina is still beautiful, alluring, and can wind men round her little finger, including at times her son. She is also stingy, self-dramatising and self-indulgent. Here they are quarrelling over Trigorin.

> KONSTANTIN ...These last few days I've loved you as tenderly and whole-heartedly as I did when I was a child. I've no one left apart from you. But why, why has that man come between us?

ARKADINA   Konstantin, you don't understand him. He's someone of the highest integrity ...

KONSTANTIN   However, when they told him I was going to challenge him to a duel his integrity didn't hinder his cowardice. He's leaving. Ignominiously fleeing!

ARKADINA   Oh, nonsense! I'm taking him away. You can't be pleased by our relationship, of course, but you're perfectly intelligent, and I must insist that you respect my freedom.

KONSTANTIN   I do respect your freedom, but you must allow me to be free too, you must let me have my own opinion of that man. Someone of the highest integrity! Here we are on the point of quarrelling over him while he sits in the drawing room or the garden somewhere laughing at us... Educating Nina, trying to convince her once and for all that he's a genius.

ARKADINA   You take pleasure in being disagreeable to me. That man is someone I have great respect for, and I must ask you not to speak ill of him in my presence.

KONSTANTIN   I don't have great respect for him, however. You want me to think he's a genius as well, but I'm sorry, I can't tell a lie – his work nauseates me.

ARKADINA   That's jealousy. People with no talent themselves, only pretensions, are always reduced to running down people who do have real talent. It must be a great comfort!

KONSTANTIN   (*Ironically*). Real talent! (*Furiously*) I've more talent than the lot of you, if it comes to that! (*tears the bandage off his head*) You and your dull, plodding friends have got a strangle-hold on art, and the only things you consider legitimate and real are the ones you do yourselves – everything else you crush and smother! I don't acknowledge any of you! I don't acknowledge you, I don't acknowledge him!

ARKADINA   And what are you? A Decadent!

KONSTANTIN   Go off to your nice little theatre and act in your miserable mediocre plays!

ARKADINA   I've never acted in plays like that in my life! Leave me alone! You couldn't write so much as a miserable farce! You shopkeeper! Yes – Kiev shopkeeper! Parasite!

KONSTANTIN   Miser!

ARKADINA   Ragbag!
(*Konstantin sits down and weeps quietly.*)
Nonentity! (*Passing to agitation*) Don't cry. There's no need to cry... (*Weeps*) You musn't cry...

Susan Fleetwood and Simon Russell Beale in the RSC production of **The Seagull**.

There is more to the playing of this scene than simply feeling and understanding the interplay of character, intention and emotion. It is a furious quarrel, and they both become very angry, but the over-all effect of their rowing is to make us laugh. Look closely at the lines and you'll find that they both express themselves rhetorically, elaborately, theatrically; despite the strong emotions they both feel, they can't help turning a scene from life into a scene from a play. Arkadina is an actress to the core of her being, and cannot use language in any other way, and Konstantin as a would-be writer not only has some of her talent for 'scenes' but is fascinated by high-flown language; he regards the language of the theatre of his time as banal, and in his attempt to write something better, has created a little play which is obscure, arty and grandiose. The difficulty in playing these two characters is in making sure they don't topple over into 'hamminess', since they both mean what they say, or have convinced themselves that they do. They both use words with great skill, to manipulate each other's emotions, but finally it disintegrates into a fine, vulgar slanging-match. All the technical skills discussed in the last chapter are needed here: energy, lots of breath and good breath control, since they both use long eloquent sentences, phrase following phrase without many pauses; finesse in stressing and inflection, since it's also a Ciceronian debate, where each is trying to prevail by having the last, irrefutable word. In the case of Arkadina, we're hearing the thrilling voice and exquisite speech of the great actress who has charmed and excited half Europe for twenty years – so the actress playing her has to decide very clearly how she does it. This is a woman who has raised behaviour, speech and the expression of emotion to a high level of artifice: princes and men of distinction have languished for her. Yet in her exists something of the tarty fishwife, and in her son there is a sad yet comic mixture of noble votary, scruffy Adonis, sarcastic little bastard, and sobbing school-boy. He's twenty-five going on seventeen.

Acting the scene
Like the rest of the play, it must be rehearsed until their tempestuous behaviour and highly developed use of speech and language looks and sounds *entirely natural*: that's *THEM*. Don't forget that they think they are simply having a conversation. Let's look at the text again, with some explanation and direction.

KONSTANTIN   (It's an uncalculated, but clever and touching appeal, low-voiced; seeming to control the emotion with difficulty.)... These last few days I've loved you as tenderly and whole-heartedly as I did when I was a child. (Softly) I've no one left apart from you. (A pause. He looks at her. Konstantin quite unconsciously is very good at The Old Moody. With sad desperation.) But why ... *why* has *that man* come between us?

ARKADINA   (In her gentlest pleading voice, playing the same game) Konstantin ... you don't understand him. (Takes his

KONSTANTIN   hands in hers.) He's someone of the highest integrity...
(Exasperated by 'integrity' – he thinks only he possesses that virtue. After a very brief pause he swoops: strongly, dramatically.) However, when they told him I was going to challenge him to a duel, his *integrity* didn't hinder his cowardice! (Enunciating the words sarcastically.) He's leaving. *Ignominiously fleeing!* (He folds his arms triumphantly. The speech should be rapid, with upward inflections, he thinks he's had the last word.)

ARKADINA   (Momentarily absolutely honest, meaning You Stupid Boy) Oh nonsense! I'm taking him away. (Konstantin snorts, then Arkadina speaks rapidly and more formally) You can't be pleased by our relationship, of course, but you're perfectly intelligent, and I must insist that you respect my freedom. (Arkadina is agile and fluent: she can change from winning mother to chilling great lady in mid-speech; here she does it by articulating the consonants with just a tiny bit more clarity: '*respect my freedom*'.)

KONSTANTIN   (Strongly, rapidly, 'topping' her.) I do respect your freedom, but you must allow me to be free too, you *must* allow me to have my own opinion of that man. (The pauses shown by the commas are very short. Konstantin's mood is revealed by his pace.) (With heavy sarcasm) Someone of the highest integrity! (He sees that his rhetoric isn't working, so he gets off his high horse, and speaks flatly, rapidly, ironically.) Here we are on the point of quarrelling over him while he sits in the drawing room or the garden somewhere laughing at us... (All on one breath.) *Educating* Nina,/trying to convince her/once and for all/ that he's a genius (I've broken the last sentence into phrases, because it seems 'that he's a genius' could be thrown away, said rapidly and diminuendo. Konstantin when he's in full flood can easily be played over-emphatically, and if he is he becomes an unspontaneous bore, just a pushy young phoney and emotional greedyguts. You can see how a mistake in vocal strategy can completely change the audience's perception of a character.)

ARKADINA   (A martyr, her goodness flung in her teeth by an unnatural monster of a son.) You take pleasure in being... (Picking the word, with a little shudder) *disagreeable* to me. (Still being formal, the great lady) That man is someone I have great respect for, and I must ask you not to speak ill of him in my presence. (The difficulty with Arkadina is that she mustn't seem a self-dramatising poseuse: she is an utterly convincing actress from moment to moment, most especially when expressing her apparently deep and rich emotions.)

KONSTANTIN (In for what he thinks is the kill) *I* don't have great respect for him, however. You want me to think he's a genius as well, but I'm sorry (Never was anyone *less* sorry), I can't tell a lie – his work nauseates me. (Punch line at the end of the speech. It's forceful and sarcastic, and needs plenty of breath.)

ARKADINA (At last the woman is taking over from the actress and she flares up) That's jealousy! People with no talent themselves, only *pretensions*, are always reduced to running down people who *do* have real talent. It must be a great comfort! (A mouthful, delivered rapidly, forcefully – verbal fencing.)

KONSTANTIN (Ironically.) REAL TALENT! (Furiously; she's hit him where it hurts most, and he's losing control.) I've more talent than the lot of you, if it comes to that! (Tears the bandage off his head. It's a rather silly turban-like bandage, concealing the superficial wound from his previous attempt to shoot himself. This is comedy on the brink of sadness and despair. Arkadina, true to form, has pinned it up with a flashy piece of costume jewellery. How can you have a proper, serious family row when you look a right nerd? He speaks quickly and passionately, but doesn't lose control of the *words*, it's lethally coherent) You and your dull, plodding friends (She gives a gasp of rage) have got a stranglehold on art, and the only things you consider legitimate and real are the ones you do yourselves – everything else you crush and smother! (Another mouthful, needing a lot of breath, it's spoken quite loudly, and with some intensity. Again the speech gets stronger toward the end.) I DON'T ACKNOWLEDGE ANY OF YOU! (Big breath) I DON'T ACKNOWLEDGE HIM!

ARKADINA (Rapidly, with great intensity and precision) And-what-are-you? (A pause, then a majestic roar) A DECADENT!

KONSTANTIN (A horrified huge breath, then low, fast, and furiously) Go off to your nice little theatre and act in your miserable mediocre plays!

ARKADINA (After a minute pause to register what he's said, then quickly, emphatically, enraged – all in one breath, running the words together)

I've never acted in plays like that in my life! Leave me alone! (Tiny pause) You couldn't write so much as a miserable farce! (Louder) You ... SHOPKEEPER! (She picks the word for maximum insulting effect; again, in triumph) Yes! KIEV shopkeeper! (A tiny pause, then) PARASITE! (She screams the word.)

KONSTANTIN (Gibbers, then:) MISER!

ARKADINA (A great cannon taking aim) RRAAGGBBAAGG! (She uses the great voice and abrasive articulation that can quell half a thousand vodka-soaked punters in Novosibirsk. Konstantin's face crumples. He sits like a collapsing ghost in a white sheet. A pause as she refuels. Then, slowly, in her most basso note:) N O N ... EN TI TY.... (A pause. She looks at the weeping Konstantin, a pause, then tearfully:) Don't cry! (He gives a wailing sniffle.) There's no need to cry! (They both sob noisily for a moment.)

A very funny scene, but demanding a lot of skill and vocal resources from the actors. In a translation into English, the nearest equivalent accent in terms of a character's education, occupation and social class should be used, which means most subtle R.P. For American actors, there is an alternative, the accents of the wealthy and cultured classes would be appropriate. Somewhere in the Deep South, perhaps? Or Philadelphia or Boston? Whatever is chosen, the audience must find the mode of speech recognisable, likely and consistent. A version of this play by the Irish dramatist Brian Friel uses Irish speech rhythms and figures of speech, and: the family are transposed into the Anglo-Irish upper classes. Arkadina's speech is that of the accomplished middle-aged middle-class actress as we would understand one: Maggie Smith, Vanessa Redgrave, Judi Dench and Joan Plowright spring to mind. He speaks with the skill of a young man who has been educated at one of the major public schools, who could after all be an odd-ball and a failure. They are both Romantics and sentimentalists, and love the sound of their own voices; and they both blur the boundary between life and art.

Speaking Skills: a Summary

Let's recap on some of the technical skills that we need to use, which have emerged from the four scenes examined, and look at a number of others we have not yet considered. This is not the whole sum of what the actor does with speech, and many more examples will come up in other chapters, because all acting has to be thought of as a piece; it isn't a series of processes that you apply one after the other.

Inflection The way we vary speech to convey an *exact* meaning: the voice and speech moving, the note rising or falling, loud, soft, or in-between. Variation of speed, rhythm and use of pause, from the tiny beat to the long deliberate pause, when you want the audience to think. Subtle differences of articulation when someone is speaking precisely and also speaking flowingly and naturally.

Stress words The more natural the speaking, the more calm the mood, the fewer words are stressed. The same can apply to emotion-laden speech of great importance. Two movie stars playing the dialogue leading up to the great shoot-out in a really fine Western are going to stress very little, and speak evenly and laconically. Heroes and villains always do. The guy who is too emphatic is usually the one who gets shot. The actor's aim is only to stress or emphasise the *essential* words to convey meaning. Over-stressing is a device used by bad actors to get a laugh out of an audience of foreigners. The aim of all stress is to make sense of meaning and emotion in the right way for the scene and situation.

Topping Taking over the line of the dialogue, either by picking up the point, or interrupting a line of thought. '...I insist that you respect my freedom...' 'I DO RESPECT YOUR FREEDOM...' The actors top by coming in louder or with greater intensity, perhaps faster, and by timing exactly. It's a piece of vocal agility.

Phrasing and tempo 'Phrasing', like 'rhythm' is one of those words directors like to use when they haven't the faintest idea how the actor should convey meaning, but they hope he will somehow stumble across it. Phrasing is part of inflection, finding the smallest groups of words that belong together, and relating them to the rest of what is said: However/ when they told him/ I was going to challenge/ him to a duel/ his integrity/ didn't hinder his cowardice/...'

Tempo is an overall effect of pace. The tension in the scene from *The Caretaker* is created by tempo; Mick is in charge of time, and can speak when he wants to, can keep Davies waiting, or rush and hassle him. In the scene from *The Seagull*, the tempo is at first careful and reflective, but gradually accelerates during the conversation to the climax at the end – 'RAGBAG!' 'MISER!'

Laughter

Probably the hardest first entrance an actor can be asked to make is to enter, laughing heartily. There's some comfort if it has to be done with other actors, in that there's safety in numbers, but solo laughter can be a martyrdom. The first thing to establish is that it has absolutely nothing to do with the actor's own emotions, just as seeming to be in a blind fury needs an actor in full control of his faculties, not an actor consumed with anger. A laughing actor is not amused by the lines that make his character laugh, as he's heard them again and again during rehearsals and performances: the cast have long since stopped chuckling at the funny lines (and what if they're *not* funny?). So laughter is a brave and generous act, like warmth and relaxed smiling. Generations of directors have hissed 'eyes and teeth' to thousands of actors required to enter, smiling brightly. Laughter is an explosive, sudden reaction, which most often appears to release a gale of emotion: sometimes it is laughter which is palpably false, or ironic, and so has an opposite meaning to true laughter, which *must* seem to be spontaneous. Laughter is a mini-language, which merely by making those noises, can convey a multitude of states of mind and meanings, from the sibilant snigger of the dangerous nutter to the delightful spifflicated giggle of someone who dare not show her mirth, from the harsh laughter of cruel triumph to the roars of genuine honest mirth.

An actor in action is working very hard, whilst often appearing to be light-hearted, at ease, physically relaxed. He or she is physically relaxed, the key to lightness and humour, and an actor and an actress playing a scene of delightful funny friendship and flirtation, full of varying kinds of laughter are playing the most technically demanding kind of dialogue: chortles, giggles and chuckles need to be as perfectly timed as words. Laughter communicates itself to the audience; the actor laughing invariably makes *them* laugh. Any kind of tension or nervousness is going to make laughing difficult, since the sound is produced by rapid pulsations of the diaphragm. You remember the vowel sound exercise in the previous chapter, Ha He Ha Hoo etc.? Take a deep breath and say hahahahahahah as rapidly as you can, then hohohhohohoh, followed by hehehehehehehe and heehee-heeheeheeheeh. It sounds like a prescription for how to play characters in pantomime or caricature stage villains. The object of the exercise, which must be persistently worked on, is to make the diaphragm *automatically responsive*. Just as the smile of the public figure flashes out when it's the hundredth hospital ward she's opened this year.

Laughter has its own inflections: pitch, tempo, loudness and softness, so the actor must experiment with variety, as no two people laugh alike. It's a familiar stage trick to make sycophants and crawlers echo, sound for sound, the laughter of the person they are flattering. Probably the greatest test of the 'laugher' is the 'laughing song' from opera or vaudeville, and the great vocal comedian Stan Freeberg has recorded a virtuoso number, rather unkindly titled 'I laughed at your wedding' where he uses just about every kind of laughter. It's utterly hilarious – I recommend every actor to have it in his collection and play it every three months.

So laughter is another adroit technical process requiring mastery of the machine, though by now you may be feeling that with such a solemn approach to the whole thing, you'll never be able to deliver the goods. As a celebrated great actor said to his gifted but earnest co-star, why don't you just try acting? The laughing actor's reward is in his sense of his own skill and that of his fellow actors, and in the laughter of the audience.

5
Body and Movement

We walk to the centre of a stage, or the camera pans with us across a studio set. Before we say a single word we've sent several messages that the audience can understand: our state of health, energy, athleticism, appetites, mood, age and situation. Not all of these register at once, but some of them are conveyed. When the actor speaks and lives on the stage or screen his body supports and helps explain that character, that person. Sometimes the body is the most apparent characteristic of that person. Shakespeare's Sir John Falstaff is above all else, *fat:* Jokes are made about his fatness: ...for reveng'd I will be, as sure as his guts are made of puddings.' Most of the time the fat knight is played by a tall, strong, athletic actor, suitably padded and whiskered, as it's a very busy part and he has a lot of physical things to do. Body shape and the way in which you move is part of your personality and Falstaff's obesity conditions his life. The paradox in his case is that within that massive bulk there is an elegant, courtly, thin man fighting to get out, and it is emotionally and dramatically interesting if he has nimble legs and feet, expressive and delicate hands, and, when not debilitated by food, drink or sheer exertion, a gracefulness of posture and movement. Though he's a prudent coward, a great toper and glutton, and a boastful liar, he is a lovable man because he has a witty, generous and graceful personality. So what he is in poundage, and *how he lives* in that great body with so much joie de vivre is the essence of him. To play him as a clumsy man or a potential hospital case would not seem to correspond with Shakespeare's intentions.

The late Hattie Jacques, she of so many television sitcoms and all the *Carry On* films, played a great number of romantic, amorous and ultra-feminine women, always rebuffed, but always hopeful. She was a statuesque woman, indeed, quite fat. But a pretty woman with sex-appeal; to see an unattractive woman enduring such humiliations would have been too cruel. The secret of her resilience and our belief that she would not only survive, but in five minutes would be cooing another man into her voluptuous embraces, lay in her elegance and agility. Always prettily shod, immaculately turned-out, she possessed the mobility of an athletic girl, and a talent for small and delicate actions. Perhaps the secret was that she was always in control of her centre of gravity, and high heels or no, always knew what her feet were doing. Someone said recently 'Comedy begins with the feet', and this could be extended to 'Acting begins with the feet'. Another fine figure of a lass, the droll and hilarious Victoria Wood, does nearly everything, including telling jokes, singing and playing the piano, with delicate lightness and precision. I have a feeling she knows what she can and can't do.

Your Body

You exist and live inside your body. You must enjoy it, and be aware of it. You must train your body, that is your physical being, to respond effortlessly to the needs of acting, to respond creatively, emotionally, imaginatively, not merely mechanically since every performance, every take is slightly different. So what you do, and how you move must emerge from motivation, the why of your characterisation, and you must be capable of adjusting to other actors. In the case of screen acting, you will need to be able to be repeat everything you do accurately.

Start with the idea of the naked body. Clothes and costume won't act for you, they are a sort of advertisement for the character you are, making an immediate statement which the actor follows up by living the physical life of that person. We live in an age of strange opposites; on the one hand, ordinary people in all their diversity have never been so well represented in film and screen, in all their beauty, ordinariness and ugliness, yet advertising and merchandising have created an alternative mythology of style. A look at TV commercials and newspaper advertising will confirm this uneasy impression: if you don't wear those jeans no man will ever look at you, if you don't drink those foaming pints you won't get a second glance from the pretty girls at the other end of the bar. These implicit pressures are something we all have to contend with, and they often make the young actor very self-conscious about what he or she actually looks like, and prone to disguise themselves. They may find themselves putting on a shell rather than working from the magnificent moving or reposeful naked body.

So start by looking at yourself naked when you get out of the bath. Calmly, kindly, and objectively. If you note something you don't like, can you do anything about it? Weight? It's very likely that you can take some off with sensible and nutritious dieting. Harder to put it on, since if you're skinny it's probably the result of your metabolism, and however much you eat you won't put on fat, but it is possible to build up muscle and solid bulk. Muscle tone? Cellulite and flab? Good muscle tone is synonymous with health, and health is attractive, as well as a necessity for the actor, whose irregular hours, sporadic eating, and time in the pub don't add up to a healthy lifestyle. Good muscle tone makes for good skin tone; you can look after the skin, and that doesn't mean a burnt-on tan acquired from a sunbed. Hair? Clean? The right length? You can do nothing much about the length of your legs, or the size of your bust, and most cosmetic surgery is of dubious value and great expense. If having a nose job will make you a happier and more confident person it may be worth the great expense, but the great screen beauty Sylvana Mangano sported a long and positively piercing nose in many films, and no one minded. So you aim to be able to look at the naked you and think, what a radiant, healthy and contented person I look. You then have to learn how to adorn that body with the right clothes, those that enhance your best features and disguise the worst. A big huggy-bear of the Robbie Coltrane persuasion could wear big dramatic clothes, and a petite woman with good ankles absolutely stunning shoes.

The modern actor no longer needs to conform to 'standards' of beauty or looks. Attractiveness is a matter of personality: health, grooming, posture, warmth and generosity of spirit. The actor's body is his machine, home, temple, goods and stock. So, without being narcissistic, love and respect it, and change anything that can be changed with self-discipline and some effort. Health, energy, agility and gracefulness are what makes an attractive, watchable actor.

The Essentials of Movement

These are: mobility and freedom, flexibility and elasticity; lightness and weight; strength and non-resistance; shape and stance, with all the parts of the body in the right place; balance and rhythm; economy and repose. The actor, whatever his or her build, is an athlete of a kind – not performing feats of strength, speed or great agility, but carrying out hundreds of everyday actions believably, to exactly the right degree. Just as he doesn't put extra words into the lines, or make superfluous noises of the er-ooh-ah-yeah kind, so he only does what is necessary. Many years ago a notorious production of Chekhov's *Three Sisters* incorporated a great deal of fidgeting, gesticulating, armpit-scratching and posturing in the cause of naturalism, the justification being that in reality, people do these very things. Musicians sometimes blow or bow wrong or bad notes during rehearsal, but woe betide them if they haven't been corrected or eliminated by performance time. All movement and action and physical conditions have a reason, which has to be discovered in text, character and relationships. The movement of an actor during a play or a screenplay is a narrative of that character's physical action and life, and is sometimes as important as dialogue; it may be a substitute for words. Each and every part of the body can be expressive, and help to create an element of character; consider a man swaggering around, dancing lightly on the balls of his feet, those feet splayed outward – they speak volumes about his character light, exuberant, witty, conceited, frivolous perhaps.

We must educate our body, its muscles, skeleton and nerves, to respond to the needs of acting. This is a long process, and like the training of the voice and speech should be given some time every day. An audience watching an actor moving and being has no conception of the immense amount of work that lies behind that dynamic energy or that casual elegance.

Some exercises toward the essentials

The professional actor in training takes from three to five movement classes a week for some three years, to train the machine and learn movement skills, including dancing, from period dance and movement to modern and tap, and other physical skills, including stage fighting, mime, acrobatics and clowning. The following suggestions are basic exercises only, and the student should follow-up by going to movement classes.

The spine The spine is the core of all movement, the central armature of our physical structure, and determines our human form. The shape and position of the spine also convey visual signals to the audience about a character's condition and state of mind; compare the bent and compressed spine of an old weary peasant woman with the whippy, proud, elegantly and seductively curved back of the ballerina. The following exercises must be done gently, not forcefully. Stop immediately if there is great strain or discomfort.

1 From the relaxation process from Chapter 3. Stand upright and let the head fall gently onto the chest; let the spine slowly melt from the top. Allow the arms to hang freely. As the body curves down let your knees bend slightly. Now breathe in and stretch upward with your

whole body and arms, but don't look upward, just let your head rock gently on the top of its column. Repeat this several times, trying to feel where your spine is; a man with a belly may become aware that his back is permanently hollowed from the weight of that gut, and an actor with poor sight may find that his head is craned forward on his neck.

2 You need to build strength and flexibility. It requires supple musculature to keep the spine straight, though not rigidly straight, as it's a flexible string of bobbins with elastic pads in between. The spine curves slightly in three places: a convex curve from mid-back to neck, a concave curve in mid-back, and another convexity as the tail, or coccyx curls under the pelvis. You strengthen the spinal muscles by using them. Do this version of a sit-up. Sit on the floor, with the legs spread slightly, knees slightly bent and let the upper body fall gently forward as in the previous exercise. Breathe in slowly and uncurl the body until it's upright. Waggle the head on a vertical axis gently from side to side; now let the spine melt from the bottom until your whole spine is as flat as it can be on the floor. Repeat this a number of times, trying to make the process quicker and smoother.

3 Kneel on all fours. Arch your back as high as you can, like a cat, position of the spine by raising your head as high as you can and sticking your tail in the air to make the deepest possible hollow in the back. Now slowly raise the middle back and lower the head until the back is absolutely level and flat and your neck is in line with the spine. Repeat this arching and curving exercise slowly, gradually increasing speed. Remember that all strengthening and flexing exercises for the back and spine must be smooth, not jerky. These have a lot in common with the exercises prescribed by physiotherapists for rheumatic conditions of the spine.

4 Where's your pelvis? A vivid image is of a bejeaned girl, standing with one hip thrust out; another is of a beer-bellied lad with a hollow back, waddling home from the pub. Both of these are inelegant postures, since the support for the part of the body for standing, walking, sitting, dancing, the pelvis, is unnaturally tilted, and the muscles which should ensure that the pelvis is mobile but in the right position have become adapted to a wrong position. Just as comedy starts with the feet, love scenes and embraces start with the pelvis, apparently in contact with another pelvis, and lips only appear to touch – that is, there musn't be a transfer of make up from one to another. The screen kiss is another matter altogether, and usually has to be a real smacker.

Try the following exercise.

Wearing only a leotard, stand in front of a long mirror, facing it, the feet about twelve inches apart. Feel the floor with your feet, toes, heels, and the ball of the foot. Now look at yourself; is one hip sticking out more than the other? Are your shoulders level? If not, flex your hips till you are in alignment and turn sideways. Hollow your back and lift your tail up as far as you can, at the same time lifting the head and arching it back, and bending slightly at the knees. Very slowly curve the spine in the opposite direction, let the head fall forward, tuck the tail under, and let the back shape into a convex curve. Hold this position for a moment and as you take a deep breath, gently straighten up from the head and down the spine, and straighten the legs, thinking the pelvis into that neat, tucked-under position. Now bend the knees, letting your body down vertically, remembering to keep the spine and pelvis in the same position as when standing. Now with your thigh muscles, rise to a standing position. Repeat this exercise several times, regularly.

Shoulders and head We've seen how the head carries sense and meaning, so the shoulders and neck must be free, poised and flexible. All gesture and action with the arms and hands flow freely from the centre of the upper chest. Try this small experiment to get the feel of this.

1 Raise your arms and elbows to the level of your shoulders, and stretch your arms out sideways, fingers spread out. Now start to curl your arms toward your chest from the fingertips; wrists, elbows, till your knuckles are pressing on your breastbone. Slowly reverse the motion, uncurling first the shoulders, then the elbows, then the wrists, and finally the hands and fingers, then back again to the closed position. You can see how the gesture involves the whole upper body. Try it again with only one arm, this time grasping an imaginary feather, which you clutch to your breast. Now with the other arm imagine you are pulling on a rope with someone pulling the other end of it.

2 To loosen the shoulders, stand with your feet apart, and check the position of pelvis and spine. Let the head float up, remembering that light, steely cord that runs through the spine from the top of your head.

Raise both shoulders as high as you can. Drop them, feeling the arms completely free. Raise and drop each shoulder alternately, making sure that there are no tensions anywhere else in the body. *The aim of all work on the body and movement is to be able to use parts of it in isolation* – a mere expressionless shrug is sometimes worth a page of dialogue. Pull both shoulders forward, letting the arms just

simply hang; now pull them backward, now each shoulder separately forward and backward. Repeat all these exercises several times,
then let the shoulders return to their true position, neither braced
back or hunched forward. The appearance of tension in the shoulders
is the most obvious sign of a nervous actor and is an impediment to
action with the top half of the body, head, arms and hands.

Weight and lightness

Every part of the body returns to its natural position because of
gravity; raise an arm and let it fall. It can fall with a bang and a slap,
or it can fall as lightly as a feather fan. The whole body can fall slowly
and gently, melting to the floor, or it can fall with a crash (the most
difficult and dangerous type of fall). Walking, sitting, rising, handling
objects, touching people, all involve the muscular effort of raising,
the effortless passivity of falling, and the sense of resistance in controlling both lowering and falling. The actor must be acutely aware of
his centre of gravity; for round that point everything happens. Bob
Hoskins playing the great clown Grimaldi made his first entrance
with several slow, perfect light cartwheels, rotating round his own
'centre': a perfect example through stylised movements of the
clown's mastery of his physical world, and an example of that special
dimension of the actor's art, *performance.* Most acting is not what it
seems to be. 'Being natural' – to Grimaldi being natural was performing remarkable actions apparently effortlessly. So the sense of
balance is essential to the appearance of lightness and heaviness.

Try these few simple exercises to feel out the movement of weight
and your centre of gravity.

1 Stand with one foot advanced about two feet. Keeping your torso
and head upright, transfer your weight to the back leg, bending the
knee of that leg a little. Now, still keeping the body upright, bring the
whole weight of your body forward over your front foot, bending the
front leg, so that you end up in a position like a swordsman's lunge.
Repeat the exercise with the feet as far apart as possible, then move
the feet gradually closer together, so that the transfer of weight from
leg to leg means only a very small movement.

2 Now stand with the feet wide apart; transfer your weight first to
one side, then slowly bring your weight to the other side, over the
other leg. Repeat, with the feet closer together. During these two exercises you will find out two things, that an actor needs strong thighs,
and that you must 'feel' the floor under you with the whole of the
foot, since the small and subtle changes of weight are made by the
slightest of pressures from the ball of the foot. A standing or moving

actor should ideally be carrying all his or her weight on the balls of the feet, the heels touching the floor as lightly as possible, so the actor needs strong and supple calves as well.

A picture is emerging of the actor as quite an athlete, performing ordinary acts with lightness and agility, strength and economy, in command of his 'centre', with all movement and gesture flowing from that point. Try this exercise for lightness.

3 Stand with the feet slightly apart, and be aware of the comfort of your whole body; shoulders, spine, pelvis all in the right place, arms hanging easily, head relaxed, eyes looking forward. Check that the legs are straight but not taut or braced, flex the knees a little. Now go into as low a knees-bend position as is comfortable, breathing easily and rhythmically. Take a deep breath, and spring upright raising your arms above your head, propelling yourself a few inches off the floor, rebounding onto the balls of the feet. *Bounce* on your feet, bounce lightly from foot to foot, forward, backward, sideways. Don't be disappointed if at first you're heavy, clumsy and off-balance; the magical lightness of dancers is the result of long patient practice – they are in reality solid muscular men and women of about eleven and a half and eight stone respectively, with bones and sinews of steel!

Movement in Dramatic Action

The purpose of training, balancing, strengthening and freeing the body is to make it a responsive instrument which can *flow* with the creative and expressive impulses. 'Applied movement', that is, the shapes, patterns, distances and volumes that the actor creates develops out of meaning discovered in the text or script, emerging as does the vocal shape and pattern. The two should grow together, not separately. At times a part of a scene, an episode in the life of a character, can be more eloquently expressed in terms of movement, demeanour and body-language than in words. Different actors have different capacities for movement. Some are notably athletic, some solid or statuesque, some floating and light, some radiating physical beauty and sexual allure. The quality that transforms the actor physically is an elusive one, the ability to feel and understand the world of the character, the scene, the play, the film. It has to do with empathy. You must plumb the depth of your sense-memory and by all the means you can, create the things that surround your character. Direct physical things such as a sense of space, light and darkness, the temperature, the energy, sounds and rhythms which surround him or her, whether the character is in danger or in a place which delights. Feel for a trigger; sometimes a piece of costume, a prop, or even an animal can set off the process whereby you move creatively and add a bodily narrative to the verbal one. Imagine a television play where the central character is a businessman sliding into disaster in a cut-throat world; a piece of costume and a prop can help create his physical world. They could be a smart shirt-collar and necktie which constrain and strangle him, making him sweat when it's hot or when he's nervous, the necktie is a badge of perhaps spurious respectability, and for some men a symbolic halter or noose. The typical screen 'heavy scene', of crack-ups in smoke-filled rooms, usually contains at least one man who in desperation has torn open his collar and loosened his tie. The trigger-prop might be a briefcase and its terrible but precious contents. One hell of a big brief-case, expensive, initialled, a status prop from the days before the slide began. It's packed with papers, and contains his past, present, and future: worthless bonds, writs, prospectuses, promises from friends, letters from the mistress about to desert him, documents about crucifying legal wranglings. If that brief case is lost or stolen his life will spiral into chaos; he daren't let go of it.

In a different play, a woman is living in terror of a man who's deserted her and now threatens her. The trigger to her physical condition might be sound – the telephone ringing, the doorbell, a car driving up to the house at night. Each of these sounds is a catalyst to gut-wrenching emotion and to action. Let's fill out the scene a little. She's about to go to bed, it's one o'clock in the morning, the house is in the gin and Jaguar belt, and a long way from the road. She moves into the hallway to check the locks on the front door, when there is an urgent rapping on the French windows of the drawing room, which open on to the garden from the back of the house. The garden has high secure walls. The light is on in the hall, the lights are still on in the drawing room, the curtains undrawn, and the front door has two panels of stained glass in its upper half. There's great scope for some purely physical acting in this dramatic situation, so let's try to imagine how our actress might handle it. She's wearing a light gown and a nightdress.

It turns into a substantial scene, typical of a late-night television chiller-thriller, the skilled actress's bread and butter. Follow its movements carefully, because they're all dramatically necessary, for character, emotion, plot, tension and situation, and whatever the cameras do, or how the editor cuts it, it's the actress who gives it truth and life, without saying a word. I've set it out as a scenario.

She hears the rapping, starts, and freezes
Her hand tightens on the bunch of keys.
Still for a moment. Cautiously she turns her head to look in the direction of the sound.
Posture of great tension, absolutely still, listening.
She darts a look at the front door. Nothing there.
Very slowly she moves down the hall to the doorway of the drawing room.
She pauses half way and kicks off the loose slippers she's wearing, and tightens the belt of her gown.
To turn off the hall lights or not? She darts a look round the hall, a moment of indecision.
She runs quickly to the light switch, but she's a bag of nerves, and fumbles with the switch, switching the lights off and on again. In desperation she slams her whole palm over the switch, and they go off again.
She lets out a gasp, and leans against the wall, rolling her forehead against it. Her palm slides down the wall.
She turns, looks down the hallway, wearily brushes the hair out of her eyes. A grim smile.
As she approaches the drawing room door she realises it's wide open and faces the French windows. Her pace slows down. In order to switch off the lights in the drawing room she'll be framed in the doorway, a sitting duck. In nightclothes. She looks round in desperation, and protectively clasps her arms around herself.
She presses herself to the wall, head tilted sideways to listen. Another hail of rappings. Terrified, she jumps back into the hallway, chewing her knuckles in agitation.
She looks desperately round.
Sees a hall-stand with sticks in it.
She darts across the hall to pull out the stoutest stick, and knocks over the stand with a crash.
She suppresses a scream, and with a shaky hand picks up the stick, tries to grip it firmly and weighs it in her hand.
Very slowly, walking steadily, bracing herself, she returns to the doorway. If she can put out the light, she can snatch the doorkey from *inside* the room and lock the door from *her* side.
With a rush she throws herself into the room, switches out the lights, and scrabbles for the key. Drops it.
Fumbles on the floor for it, finds it. Rushes back into the hall, and tries to slam the door.
Traps the hem of her gown, wrenches frantically at it, it rips; rapidly opens the door a few inches, frees the gown, slams the door, thrusts

in the key and turns it.

Half fainting, hanging on to the door handle, she falls to her knees.

A hail of rappings on the windows.

She freezes again. A moment's pause. She jumps up quickly and rushes to the telephone.

As she's about to pick it up it rings.

Her hand hovers.

She looks up. Through the front door she can hear and see a car coming up the drive.

A set-up? Him? With accomplices? A campaign to terrify her?

She snatches up the receiver, she turns and looks back to the drawing room and nearly drops the phone as a friendly voice says rapidly 'Ruth? It's Nancy. I saw all your lights on, I was worried about you.'

Ruth lets out a huge gasp of relief, and gropes for the chair by the phone. She sits.

'Ruth, hello, Ruth, I've sent Martin and Joe over to see if you're OK.'

Several loud rings on the doorbell. In the dark hallway she can see two figures through the glass of the front door. The receiver is babbling away.

She rises slowly and warily, crouching behind the door and listens intently:

'Ruth! It's Martin and Joe. Are you there? Let us in.'

Absolutely drained, she reaches up and opens the door a few inches. Sees Martin and Joe, and slowly opens it wide. As they rush into the house, she faints. Joe catches her before she hits the floor. The phone is still squeaking away in Mickey-Mouse talk.

See next thrill-packed episode.

This scene illustrates the dramatic and expressive content that movement and action can carry, most particularly in acting for the camera, and also the skill needed to play it. Consider what it contains within probably two minutes playing time:

- Contrasts in tension and relaxation.
- Contrasts in speed of movement.
- Contrasts in body shape, from an erect position to a huddled collapsed figure.
- A wide range of intense emotional expression and body language.
- Over thirty-five moves or pieces of business, needing meticulous attention to detail. The props need skilful and exact handling – nearly dropping the phone, for example.
- An exact sense of style; as I've described the scene it sounds melo-dramatic, but it requires absolute reality and truthfulness in the play-ing. Think if the central figure were a tougher or angrier woman.

- Yet, however the character is interpreted, the actress must have a relaxed but controlled body.

Reasons for Action

First, a general observation about movement and action: do less. Every move must have a reason. That reason can be of character, situation, emotion, purpose, thought. A move can also fulfil the director's purpose of making a meaningful and interesting stage picture, but actor and director must still find a human reason for it, so business is invented, drinks poured, cigarettes fetched, flowers arranged; actors feel the need to walk about. But movement must be used with the utmost economy or it turns into an inexpressive blur of whirling, fidgeting figures. One of the signs of inexperience is when the actor doesn't quickly let the language do the work, and unnecessary movement and gesture distracts from what is being said. An example of over-physicalising a performance is when an actor 'mugs', using over-emphatic and obvious facial expressions.

There used to be a set of theatrical rules which have since been discarded. Examples of these include not moving when another character is speaking and not speaking with your back to the audience. The leading actors were expected to enter up-stage centre and strike a pose. Even acting in the classical repertoire is a more natural-looking business than it was a mere forty years ago; a joyful example of this was provided some years ago by the Royal Shakespeare company in one of the Histories (I forget which: they are dense, rich, but interminable). The stage direction is *Enter the King, with a whore, on a bed.*

Some decades ago this would have involved a grand scenic object, the bed, and two grand costumes. A great canopied bed would have moved momentously down stage, with two figures on it, like a monument to a dead duke and his lady. The RSC's version of this was thoroughly human. A scruffy palliasse was pulled rapidly on-stage, and from it jumped a very unkingly figure in his drawers, his hair tangled. His girlfriend was suitably dressed for her purpose, stark naked. With a shriek she leapt up and exited hastily.

The contemporary actor has the utmost freedom of action and the only commonsense rules that apply are do nothing which doesn't have a meaning and do nothing that draws attention away from another actor who is the focus of attention. 'Gesture' is not something which can effectively be taught, except in a rather balletic or stylised sense, as in commedia dell'arte or melodrama. Gesture must arise out of necessity, to enhance expression or to express a meaning purely on its own. It is wiser to restrain yourself from making gestures if you're not very good at them, and only to make those which arise out of absolute necessity.

Stillness and repose

Stillness or repose is not inaction, if the actor is thinking in character and within the dramatic situation – it's what I've described in Chapter 2 as 'vibrant repose'. Stillness is especially important when working for the camera, even down to stillness of the face, the head, the arms and hands. Early television drama (which terrifyingly, was live) often had uneasy moments where half of the actor's head or body would disappear out of shot, because of an involuntary movement which on stage would hardly be noticeable. In a close-up the smallest twitch of an eyebrow becomes a significant gesture. Stillness is also valuable in the long speech. Most long speeches contain important narrative or are vehicles for the development of character and emotion and the actor, well-lit, becomes a focus for the audience. Movement and gesture should only be used when absolutely necessary, perhaps to mark a change of mood – a pause before a revelation, for example. Stillness and repose can only come from the actor who is properly relaxed, so that economy of movement becomes a proper use of his energy, not a form of severe self-constraint.

Period Movement

Movement belonging to a particular historic time is often used to bring that age to life: its conditions, customs, manners, spirit and priorities. 'Period' movement may be significant when playing the comedy of manners, in plays that reflect a particular society and its ways, such as the Restoration comedies. An old play is not a museum piece, interesting only for its recreation of life in the past, but also for showing part of the organic process of the development of human society. Contemporary directors tend to seek too hard for modern parallels, which is to ignore the effect of the play *in its time.* How people lived then was an essential condition of how they thought and why they thought that way.

How much period movement, behaviour and atmosphere is present in a play or screenplay depends on several factors. First, the play itself. *Macbeth,* which is about regicide and a murderous struggle for power set in a barbaric, wind and rain-swept kingdom, is very short on ceremonies and niceties of behaviour, whilst *Love's Labour's*

Lost is a romantic and elegant play, set in a beautiful place, where Renaissance kings and princesses converse, swap brilliant jokes and make love. Next, the director's decision, made with the designer: what's it going to look like? What are the actors going to *wear?* (one of the most important things as far as the actor is concerned). This is conditioned by the budget. For years now even major British classical companies have made the compromise that unless there's a very good reason most of the characters have one costume, and, as in Shakespeare's time, the set is a machine for acting in, rather than an attempt to recreate realistically the time and place of the play. Yet the plays of the Restoration and 18th century somehow need a more realistic presentation of clothing, locale and everyday life than do Shakespeare and his contemporaries, because they are about less grand people and more day-to-day real-life events.

An historic play which contains period ceremonies and rites such as dancing and fighting will need the help of a specialist dancing teacher and fight arranger, since the actors and director can't just mug something up and hope it will work. But there is a great deal the actor can do to open his imagination to a past age, a past way of living, and gain a feeling for the spirit of the period. Pictures in galleries and books can be helpful here, as can visits to museums exhibiting clothes, furniture and weapons.

Let's look at these.

Clothes Think about their decorative quality and their practicality. Were they designed for utility or attractiveness? The people of *Macbeth* dress for the climate and their way of life, huge, warm, comfortable and durable clothes, from thick materials, furs, leather. Their clothing must allow them the means to carry weapons for immediate use. The people of *Love's Labour's Lost* dress to allure and impress – power dressing. Their clothes, too, relate to how they live.

Furniture was spartan, except for beds, which were warm and deep. Nobody but the greatest people sat on chairs with backs, so a very good upright posture was necessary to maintain one's dignity when sitting on a stool. Soft upholstery was almost non-existent in the 15th and 16th centuries, so clothes were padded to give some comfort when eating your dinner every night on a hard wooden bench. Hence the huge padded breeches for gentlemen and the padding in ladies' skirts.

Weapons Men carried weapons whenever out and about. Part of a man's education was to be able to defend himself with a sword or sword and dagger. Depending on the need, servants carried swords, clubs or staves. Every household of status armed its servants – an extraordinary state of being to us, perhaps, but dictated by living in a violent world. The rights to carry arms or weapons were severely curtailed in Europe during the mid-19th century, though in America the right to do so remains a significant issue.

These are other aspects of daily life which you may find worth pondering on.

Hygiene Supplies of fresh water and the water closet did not become common till the end of the 19th century. In the early 19th century, the famous dandy and leader of fashion Beau Brummel said that the foundation of his elegance was daily 'country washing'. An admirable idea, but most people, especially the poor people in the country, didn't have much access to clean water. Louis XIV took a bath before his courtiers and intimates once a month, and he was an extremely dainty man by the standards of his time. Cleanliness next to Godliness. Things had not improved much by the late 17th century, so people of status merely used a lot of scent, make-up and fine clothes. A suit for a courtier at Versailles, a dress for a grand lady, could cost a thousand pounds or dollars, and was worn until it rotted apart.

Sexuality and display The modern way is to show it. We have become used to male and female bodies being exhibited freely, witness the flaunted erotic icons of Hollywood. But in past ages the sexual buzz was created by different means. In the 16th and 17th centuries male sexuality and allure was emphasised by exposure of the legs showing them, dressing them to be seen, and in the Elizabethan and Jacobean period, topping them with stylised genitals in the form of the codpiece, enlarged enormously, bejewelled, beribboned. (Back to the pelvis; with all that up front, you don't need to push it.) Big shoulders, long hair, swagger. Female sexuality was expressed by the suggestion of hidden enchantments – an alluring shape with feminine characteristics exaggerated but concealed. A glimpse of leg was erotic to a degree; the Elizabethan dance 'La Volta' involved lifting the woman into the air, with tantalising glimpses of leg. Otherwise, men saw faces, hands, a lot of cleavage, and most importantly, a shape, a posture, a *deportment*.

Eating and drinking Nobody talks much about food in the modern play, though some thirty years ago many scenes were framed round 'dinner parties', where people pecked at their plates, their main purpose being to make conversation and impress each other. Talk of food or consumption of it is a serious matter in older plays, because eating, drinking, *feasting* are part of life's priorities, done for the sheer gut satisfaction of being alive. The savage chieftains at MacBeth's banquet eat with their fingers and a sharp long knife, which could cut a man's throat or reduce his dinner to gulpable portions; Lord Foppington, in Vanbrugh's *The Relapse*, says, by way of comparison:

> Why, then, ladies, from thence I go to dinner at Lacket's, and there you are so nicely and delicately serv'd, that, stap my vitals, they can compose you a dish, no bigger than a saucer, shall come to fifty shillings...

You see how important the physical world is in these two vastly differing plays, and to play either of them without careful attention to their reality would rob them of their truth and their interest.

Respect and ceremony

Prior to the 19th century plays were usually about the lives and destinies of great or rich and powerful people, and greetings and farewells accordingly imply far more than they do now. They are indicative of the status of one man compared with another, in terms of money, power and reputation, and also show how the opposite sexes regarded each other. A fine gentleman's bow was performed not only out of politeness, but to show off his clothes, his sex-appeal and manliness; it enabled him to show a fine leg. Removing his hat in particular was a sign of respect and submission. A lady's curtsey might equally be done for motives of politeness, but it also showed off her arms, face, hair, figure, and breast. Women's use of fans in the late 17th and 18th centuries was far more than a matter of cooling themselves. The fan had a language of stylised gestures, meaning 'you can make a pass at me now', 'spare my blushes', 'not on your life', and so on. It was useful to hide behind, for rapping gropers over the knuckles, and for whispering to friends. In polite society it was an essential prop for a woman of fashion.

So it's a matter of 'do it properly' if it is to be done at all, and this means research and getting advice. Don't get carried away, because a play must not turn into an exhibition of bowing and scraping. But do your homework, and be true to the period and style you're playing in, since polite manners are subject to the fashion and mood of the times. There are a number of excellent books with illustrations and drawings which you can consult. (See booklist, p. 179)

The Active Actor

All bodily skills are useful to an actor. Tumbling, mime, dance, modern and tap, stage fighting (for women also; see an episode or two of *The Bill*, *Hill Street Blues* or much present-day action television). Juggling, gymnastics, swimming, riding, even martial arts may be helpful to a part. So if you have any talent for these, keep up those skills, or aim to acquire at least some of them. Acting is a life-long job, and you never know when they may come in handy.

Becoming the Character: Thought to Action

Let's try to summarise what happens during the process that leads the actor from ideas, understandings and intuitions to the full physical realisation of a character. These may vary from 'he's a dancing athletic tough guy who clowns a lot' (Mike, in Berkoff's *East*) to 'She's elegant, magnificent, stately, and everything she does is calculated for effect' (Lady Bracknell, the grand dowager in *The Importance of being Earnest*.) Two conditions must be established to help the actor to be a creative physical performer: first, that whatever the demands of the part, the actor is *truly relaxed*, something that has to be stated over and over again. From this state springs economy of movement, expressiveness and simplicity. The actor Robert Lindsay demonstrated this in the television series *G.B.H.*, a funny political satire by Alan Bleasdale. His character was a manic, ambitious, fast-talking local politician, an opportunist and greedy crook, whose chosen public persona was that of an amusing and laid-back sophisticate. Gradually, as the pressures mount on him, Murray, the character, begins to disintegrate, mentally, verbally and physically, and becomes a mass of uncoordinated jumps, dartings, tics and twitches, body language that told us volumes. The great skill of Lindsay's performance was that this bodily falling apart was done with absolute fluidity and lightness, perfect coordination of miscoordination. The impression was of a man of straw blowing apart, the dissolving of a man whose personality was a total sham. This is a very good example of the need for beautiful coordination and complete relaxation when playing a neurotic and buffeted character.

So the actor must work hard and exercise for control and flexibility of all parts of the body, separately and together; meaning may be conveyed with the entire body or merely the raising of an eyebrow. Suppleness, strength, balance, a sense of weight and also of lightness, knowing where your centre is are all important. The body must be able to respond to the thought and the instinct, to be able to *act* and *re-act*. The attention you give to your physical abilities will help you to be a better, more watchable actor of greater range. Parallel with these skills are the qualities of *repose* and economy. The actor can only succeed with demeanour, body language, facial expression and physical actions where these have a meaning derived from the text, arising truly from character and situation. Compare two kinds of action, the egregious Beverly from *Abigail's Party* giving her hilarious demo of how to put on and wear lipstick, and Lady Macbeth's sleepwalking scene, where the most important action is her hand-washing: the hands writhe and tear and fret at each other in the attempt to remove that damning, eternal blood.

True and telling visual images are vitally important. We must create the physical world of our characters, especially in the historical play, the story of people whose climate, habits and customs are different from ours. They are specific people in a particular place and time, not human stereotypes. In Noël Coward's *Present Laughter,* a comedy of the 1940s, there is a minor character, Henry Lypiatt, a West End impresario. Apart from a certain acerbic wit and ruthlessness, he is more of a function than a character, and doesn't have a lot of dialogue. A thankless chore for the actor, you may think, but he is a man of his time, when actors were still gentlemanly and flamboyant (which often concealed private lives of some seaminess) and impresarios were actors writ large: figures of awesome power, masters of the revels. So perhaps the actor might go nap on Henry's clothes, demeanour and manners. An immaculate suit, in a rather risqué colour, a French or Italian suit, horror of horrors! The lapels are too wide, the turn-ups too deep! And, my dears, he's got a *gardenia* in his buttonhole! A wide-brimmed velvet hat, like the brigand-hero of an opera; very tight, very expensive gloves; an exquisite pale floral silk necktie and beautiful two-tone shoes. He smokes oval Turkish cigarettes in a long black holder and carries a silver-topped cane. His ever-charged cigarette-holder, except when he raises it to his lips, is held most precisely at least a foot away from his body, so that his clothes and person shall not be contaminated by smoke; it's also a Field Marshal's baton with which he makes imperious gestures. An amusing epicene figure of authority and considerable interest, achieved by the actor's attention to the details of physical presentation, and a creature who by his physical presence evokes a feeling of the theatre and the period. A man precisely in his time and place.

In short, the use of costume, body and movement completes and rounds off a performance, and must be as full of truthful insight as the actor's speech.

6
Rehearsals

Rehearsal time is when performances are created, an organic growing process when anything can happen, when different things happen in an unpredictable way, when actors make progress at different speeds. It's not apparently very systematic, not a steady and logical progression through the play, rather a group of people plucking memories and inspirations from deep inside themselves, and like building up a jigsaw puzzle, slowly creating story, characters and relationships. A *collective* work of creativeness.

There is never enough time in rehearsal, so use it well. When you enter the rehearsal room, your mind and feelings must be focused on the work to be done. A stage or television play usually rehearses for anything from two weeks to two months, from 10 o'clock to 5 o'clock, five, six or even seven days a week. Thirty years ago plays were frequently rehearsed for a week, and miraculously got on, often with excellent performances. The only comparable experience today is actors working in a television soap, who must be fast-thinking, responsive and quick studiers. The bigger commercial companies or the subsidised flagship theatres can sometimes afford six to eight weeks or more for big and complex projects, but three or four weeks is the average. The amateur actor usually rehearses for three or four hours at a time, somewhere between three or four times a week, so he or she has to be able to switch on the concentration very quickly, and also to remember the thoughts and feelings of a rehearsal which may have been several days ago. Knowing how to rehearse is a most important skill and results in performances rich in insight and detail. Good actors, though they continue to develop their performances, offer to their fellow actors a secure performance; they don't 'wing it', that is play lines, movements and business in an improvised way, not as rehearsed. Momentary inspiration may descend on them, but it is of no use if the rest of the cast are unable to follow them.

The Audience

We must be aware of how the audience contributes to the performance as a whole. Acting is shared with an audience, whether
they're in a theatre or sitting at home in front of their television
screens. It is a three-way relationship, between the play, the actors
and the watchers. Most actors prefer stage acting because of the live
presence of the watchers and their response whether that is of
profound interest, deep emotion or laughter. It is a fact, however, that
the audience are not only affected and moved by the actors, but that
it often assumes a collective mood, perhaps pre-disposed to laugh at
anything one particular character does or says. Sometimes an audience appears bored and uninterested. It is also true that the collective
intelligence of an audience is operating on a lower level than the
intelligence of the individual members. Whatever form an audience
takes, it is a volatile and unpredictable body.

During this century various experimenters and innovators, the
most important of whom are Brecht and Artaud, have tried to
change the way in which audiences react to the dramatic experience.
Brecht, like Shaw, was a political dramatist who criticised bad
government, injustice, oppression and corruption. Whereas Shaw
beguiles us with witty or hard-hitting dialogue, Brecht set out to
establish the 'alienation effect', whereby the audience are encour-
aged to be more objective in their judgement of the issues of the play,
and carry away positive information, a blueprint for future political
action. To achieve this, Brecht required that their emotional involvement with fictitious characters and situations should be brusquely
interrupted and that didactic factual information should be inserted
into the stream of the play. From *The Caucasian Chalk Circle*:

AZDAK   (the crafty Village Clerk who has become a Judge): War
         lost, but not for Princes. Princes have won their war. Got
         themselves paid 3,863,000 piastres for horses not deliv-
         ered, 8,240,000 piastres for food supplies not produced...

Another aspect of Brecht's approach can be illustrated briefly from the
same play. Grusche, who has taken loving charge of an orphaned child,
chucks the 'baby' into the wings after a scene of tender maternal affection (the 'baby' is a mere prop, a rolled-up blanket). This baby, and his
fate, is at the heart of the play, and must engage the concern of the
audience. Giles Havergal solved this problem brilliantly in his production, by having one of the actors accompanying Grusche everywhere
provide the baby's crying voice. The actor playing a young café waiter
was thrilled to bits with his role. At the core of Brecht's idea is that the

actor should 'demonstrate' the character, offering it up to be judged by the intelligence alone, free from the actor's emotional engagement with the audience. Time has shown that audiences don't react that way, either they are interested or they're not, but Brecht's effect on staging and dramatic writing has been immense. His short scenes, where lots of unnecessary naturalistic explanations are pruned away, and his economical but vivid characterisation are an invitation to the audience to *use their imagination*. The scene from *The Caretaker*, in Chapter 4, owes something in its sparsity to this influence and Robert Bolt has said that the structure and style of *A Man for All Seasons* was powerfully influenced by Brecht. Steven Berkoff believes above all in the power of the actor and the text, and has thought long and hard about audiences and he too shows something of Brechtian thinking:

> Imagination is the great rambling whale of the audience's mind that must be harpooned by the controlled imagination from the stage...
>
> By leaving space for the spectator, by eliminating the junk of sets and over-explained narrative the spectator can become part of it and is linked to the events by the demands of his imagination, that is interpreting *for itself* what is happening...

So Brecht has liberated us from the literal-minded longueurs of unnecessary dramatic plausibility, but we must remember that the actor must still possess and exercise skill and strategy in speech, movement, thought and emotion.

The other major influence on treaties about the connection between the actor and audience was Antonin Artaud, unsuccessful actor, eccentric playwright and madman. His views are the converse of Brecht's and he wants us above all to feel, to be transported. His concept of 'the Theatre of Cruelty' is not a prescription for sadistic acts, but for the profoundest experience of the senses, and the means he chose to create such feelings were greatly influenced by theatre and dance from other cultures, from Bali, from the East. These include strange images (his version of *The Cenci* specifies that in a banquet scene half the people present should be enacted by gigantic effigies of human beings), incantations, acrobatics, music, and strange lights, colour, costumes and make-up. A surreal, hypnotic drenching of the senses, where we abdicate judgements and surrender to feeling and sensuality. Artaud's creed has also had a profound effect on writing, staging and acting, and has led to the use of electronic sound and music, the interpolation of dance into narrative, and tremendous leaps of the imagination. *Cats* and *Starlight Express* and many modern and musical plays could not have been created and staged without the spur from Artaud.

The Director

Should be superhuman but usually isn't. We live in an age of 'director's theatre', where some directors impose a very distinctive interpretation or style on a play, sometimes with an interesting and fresh result, at other times swamping it with pretentious and unnecessary contrivances. The director's principal job is first, to interpret the play or screenplay as the writer means it; next, to organise the physical needs of the production, the mise-en-scène, costumes, lighting, sound, and to some degree the physical choreography of movement. He or she will work with the actors to make the best use of the acting space so that the audience are given a series of interesting visual images which support and enhance the meaning and moods of the piece. In the case of a naturalistic play with a small cast the director should allow the actors as far as possible to evolve their own moves, which will emerge from their relationships as dramatic characters. A large-scale show, a musical, a big cast epic or classic will need quite a lot of organisation – a crowd scene would become meaningless chaos if the director did not define clearly, who is where, and what they are doing.

Whilst the director should possess these necessary skills, his or her most important job is to *help the actors* in their search for a performance, for a character and relationships; to encourage them to be bold, to restrain them gently when they're on the wrong track, to illuminate the text for them when they're stuck, to create good relationships between them as actors. In short, to create an atmosphere of interest and excitement in which the actor feels creative but secure.

The screen director, whether for film or television, is in technical matters much more the boss, requiring the actor to use physical dimensions and space with meticulous accuracy, and to deliver a contained performance which is always thought through, sometimes over many months. Working for the camera is for the experienced actor. He or she must be well cast in terms of appearance, speech, personality and temperament. It is the job of the casting director to match the actor to the part and to present the director with a package of actors who have the technical and artistic skills to cope easily with the medium.

The actor must aim for a friendly and confident relationship with the director, accepting his or her advice and technical guidance whilst at the same time taking initiatives and being responsible for his own performance. Actor and director must agree before starting rehearsals about the general outline of the role and the character's part in the dramatic action, which doesn't, however, close the door to discoveries and revelations as rehearsal progresses. A play or screenplay melts when filtered through the imagination of the actors and their relationship with each other. A wise director watches these developments and helps the actor to select from the number of options open to him. Much of the time, actors need each other more than they need the director; they are exchanging feelings and emotions, and the director is merely there to encourage or advise on matters of dramatic emphasis – 'that line a little louder'; 'isn't he perhaps more dejected when she tells him the marriage is off?' He must always be prepared to explain simply the reason for a piece of direction, and the actor should always ask for explanation if he or she doesn't fully understand. But remember that rehearsing a play is a process of making discoveries, of rummaging in the subconscious mind, of evolving relationships. It isn't a matter of merely making a series of rational decisions, but of subtly altering performances in twenty different ways, of selecting, refining, developing. So nineteen out of twenty rehearsals are slightly wrong as the actor probes the text and draws up thoughts and feelings from his own experience. The actor must get on with it, and not get drawn in to long and fruitless discussions; it's better to work a scene half a dozen times than to talk about it for an hour.

The Production Team

Get to know the other members of the production team. The designer and costume designer will have thought about and discussed the play in depth, and as we found in the last chapter, a single item of clothing may be a trigger toward a characterisation. Maybe the designer has visited the place where the play is set: 'It was freezing cold out of doors, and very stuffy indoors' ... 'Everybody was eating, all the time, they worship food and drink and cook it and eat it in the street'. Get on good terms with the stage management team. You need them. Their job is to run the production, and they are highly skilled and highly trained, setting up and supervising rehearsal, providing props and stage furniture, documenting the moves made by the actors, integrating movement of scenery, sound effects, other effects and lighting with the live action of the actors. One assistant or deputy stage manager will be the actor's constant saviour. He or she will be 'on the book', that is, prompting during rehearsal and performance if necessary, which it shouldn't be. The ASM will remind you of moves you made at the last rehearsal, put you right if you go wrong, and after a scene has been worked, tell you where you've paraphrased the text. John Mortimer put the dramatist's point of view succinctly when he said that the playwright slaves over the typewriter striving to find exactly the right dialogue for his characters, and doesn't welcome arbitrary or sloppy changes, additions and omissions.

The Process of Rehearsal

The actor must go into rehearsal having read the whole play, however small his part; if he's got a cough and a spit, he may be lucky enough to watch some fine actors and actresses working, and have the chance to observe their skills, their methods and their mystery. Read the play carefully and form your own general impression of it.

A kindly director will make the introductions and try to put the cast at their ease. If he's a wise director he or she will say a little bit about the play, giving a general impression, perhaps that language is paramount, or that the play is an ingeniously wrought and very complex machine, or that it should look very elegant and stylish. If the director goes on at length, listen and make a discreet note or two.

It's still a common practice to have a first reading right through the play, so that the actors can form a further feeling about the play. This is usually fairly terrifying except for the old hands, who will read their way through in a most leisurely fashion as if they were having a conversation over brunch; they are trying to dig out meaning. Follow their example; don't try to impress anyone, ask questions where necessary, and above all, listen to the other actors, try to sense what sort of people they are. Perhaps for the next year you are going to act the most intimate relationships with them. The girl sitting opposite is your wife, the guy at the end of the table is your father in the play. So from the start be prepared to like them and approach them with interest, sympathy and good faith. Other directors may start rehearsals with a session of improvisation, perhaps to throw the actors into immediate relationship with each other, or for his or her own purpose – to find out more about them. An actor at a job interview is usually on his best behaviour, well-dressed and wagging his tail, and may be a different animal in the rehearsal room. Most actors prefer to find out more about the play rather than starting off with improvisation.

Blocking or Plotting

I suggested in the chapter on movement that some plays need a lot of arrangement because of the numbers of actors and the quality of visual presentation. So blocking moves can be a lengthy process. The naturalistic play about close relationships and behaviour is going to derive much of its visual impact from the characters and their physical interaction. The director may say no more than 'you enter, and find him sitting there', giving the two actors the opportunity to relate naturally to each other. Don't be afraid of this. He will gradually sort it out, deleting what's unnecessary, wrong or fidgety.

Whilst the ASM 'on the book' is documenting all the moves, it's the actor's responsibility to note down and remember his own moves, particularly in large ensemble scenes where a lot of people are moving about and positions in relation to each other, scenery and stage furnishings are critical. Some directors are notable for their ability to use actors as scenery, in the sense that a stage picture has a lot in common with the painter's imagery, and is a composition of interesting human figures. A most fascinating version of Oscar Wilde's baroque and poetic *Salome* at the Royal National Theatre used stylisation of movement to an extreme degree. The director, Steven Berkoff had decided against naturalistic movement, presumably because it would be laughably in contrast with the play's heightened language. He was also against using historical period costume, perhaps again because it would make the play look like a fustian melodrama. The actors were dressed with superb elegance in the clothes of 1920s fashionables, with the exception of the luckless John the Baptist, who wore a smart loincloth; the voluptuous Salome wore a decorous gold dress, and Berkoff himself, playing Herod, attired himself as a grand cloaked dandy, cuban-heeled and bejewelled, a figure that might have been dreamed up by the celebrated designer Erté. The actors mainly moved very slowly, as if walking underwater, so every move, every pose and position and grouping became an uncanny and surreal experience for the audience. From time to time they danced frenziedly to jazz music; Salome herself performed a most erotic Dance of the Seven Veils without removing a stitch of clothing. This was most demanding blocking, which the cast carried out with wonderful detail and control, and there can be no doubt that it evolved during the whole period of rehearsal. Similarly, musical theatre makes use of highly stylised choreography and blocking, where the actor's movement has much of the quality of dancing.

So the actor should be able to respond to two very opposing methods of putting a play into action, the first where he is allowed to do what comes naturally, which means releasing himself mentally so that what happens is real, spontaneous and full of meaning; the other approach more to fulfil the director's choreographic requirements and use a dancer-like body language of pictures and symbols.

Sometimes the two are used in the same production, for example the kids in *West Side Story* who lounge, chat, fight and feud quite realistically, then switch to highly choreographed musical scenes.

If a definite pattern of moves is given, it's probably because rehearsal time is short, or that the director has a vision of something precise that will facilitate the scene and help the actors by giving them a 'cradle' of moves. Most directors add the proviso that the actors are free to develop and change moves if they are uncomfortable and don't feel right. Aim to use space adventurously, *explore* it: follow the hunch, and respond to other actors in a human and instinctive way. Don't forget, rehearsal is a time for experiment, when you're spilling paint, moulding clay in your hands. It's not a procedure, it's a time for creation and should be fun. Inventing the physical action should also be fun.

Characterisation

I said in Chapter 1 that you can persuade the audience that you are the character, or that the character is you, add that to some extent all roles, however close they are to the real you, need characterising. In present day acting, which is very true to life, to real thought patterns, speech and behaviour, characterisation is a very subtle matter. The actor when offered a part says to himself 'Why me?' The first answer may be that in the broadest personality terms, the character is rather like the actor. The next answer might be that he or she has certain skills and aptitudes, qualities of voice, movement, personality and temperament that are useful for playing the part. Romeo should be young-looking, agile and have a lot of youthful sex-appeal, strong emotions and the openness to express them; he should also have an attractive voice, good speech, intelligence, and a sense of humour – a specification which many young male actors can fulfil. Jimmy Porter's weary and much-abused wife Alison should be able to summon up every subtle nuance of upper-middle class English speech and physical demeanour, even though her clothes and surroundings are shabby, and she hasn't had a decent hair-do in months. She must also have a quality of temperament which suggests fragility of physical and emotional health. This girl has not been prepared for the life she's leading: the lower, discontented end of the rat-race, where finally they're all losers. A difficult part to cast and play and a robustly handsome girl or a woman with an irresistible smile wouldn't be able to play her unless she could sink these qualities and suggest the fragility and polite gentle warmth of Alison.

Everyone has a different view of a play and its characters, including the actors in it. True playing of character arises from the interaction of the actors, and later the characters as they develop and relate to each other. The character the actor finally brings to performance may be very different from his original conception. Yet to begin with a series of questions must be asked and answered, since they are the foundation stones on which character is built. Most of this information can be derived from the script, what the character says about himself, or what other people say about him or her but this is not to say that you can expect to get a blueprint of the character from the text. Good dramatists don't dictate, they allow character to be *interpreted*, and often an actor develops a characterisation from a mere hint, an adjective perhaps.

Take this scene from *Once a Catholic*:

MOTHER THOMAS AQUINAS

What a foul, despicable creature you are. I'm thoroughly disgusted with you...

AND   I'm sorry, but I don't believe you. I suggest you know full well why you chose such a question. To make yourself the centre of attraction and procure a cheap laugh at Father Mullarkey's expense. The last time you were in this office you tried to hoodwink me into believing you to be an innocent girl, immature for your years ... And now I'm quite certain that you're not the least bit innocent. You're an exceedingly sophisticated girl, full of knowing beyond your years ...

Mary O'Malley's funny and charming comedy is set in a North London Convent Grammar School. She has provided us with thumbnail sketches of the characters:

Mother Thomas Aquinas – a tall, thin, fairly young and very refined Irish nun with spectacles. Headmistress ...
Mary Mooney – (the girl she's lecturing) A fifth former. She is plain and scruffy and has ginger hair, freckles and a very good soprano singing voice.

There is probably a lot of truth in Mother Thomas's assessment of Mary Mooney, who is a scheming manipulative monkey, so the actress has a lot of help from the start. All pretty girls take heart, it's perfectly possible to look plain and scruffy, and the Our Lady of Fatima knickers so lovingly described in the text are enough to take any girl's mind off sex – except that they don't. Similarly, all plain and scruffy girls take heart; glamour comes from artifice and determination. Opposite is Mary Gallagher's description of Mother Peter, another teacher.

June Page, Anna Keaveney and Jane Carr playing three of the schoolgirls from **Once a Catholic**.

She's such a crafty old cow. She makes us all learn it but she'll only pounce on one of us to test it. Whoever she happens to pick on will have to get up and act it. In front of the whole form. With her. She always gives herself the part of Lady Macbeth. God, it's so embarrassing. Especially when she puts on an English accent and doing all the fancy gestures. Every time she opens her mouth a spray of spit comes flying across the classroom ...

O'Malley's description:

Mary Gallagher – A sensible attractive dark-haired fifth former.
Mother Peter – A tall, fat, middle-aged Irish teaching nun.

The actresses can assume, then, that Mary Gallagher's description is a truthful one; she has captured the power, passion, humour and sarcasm of the formidable Mother Peter with great accuracy.

So a rich and complex text, written for the stage, is a mine of information about character. A screenplay is a different matter. In the celebrated *The Third Man* the scene is immediate post-war Vienna, ruined and bleak, under the control of the occupying powers. Rackets and corruption are the other economy – the black economy – and food, housing, fuel, tobacco, drugs and medicine are in the hands of crooks. Harry Lime is the Penicillin Baron. He appears infrequently; the first shot of him is of his immaculate and expensive shoes. He speaks the minimum of dialogue, never raises his voice, shows no emotion, and reveals nothing about himself. Yet this performance by Orson Welles is a piece of cinema history, remembered as a display of acting of awesome power; he persuaded us totally that he *was* Harry Lime, and Harry Lime was him. The characterisation was economical, a superb presence, a seductive and velvety voice, immaculate clothes, steely will, and absolute control of emotion (the only opinion he allows himself is that the genius and industry of the Swiss nation produced nothing of more distinction than the cuckoo-clock). Yet even this is only gently sarcastic. This emphasises the point that characterisation means finding a *true individuality*, not putting together a collection of personal eccentricities, tics, traits and mannerisms, and the actor must not be afraid of playing restraint and containment. It's very tempting to want to display all the possibilities, psychological and behavioural, that exist within a human being; I referred to this in Chapter 1 as empty virtuosity. The result is acting clutter.

Here are examples of some of the questions actors asks themselves as they study and work on the play. Don't forget that creating a real character is something that happens all through rehearsal; you don't go into rehearsal with your mind made up about what sort of a person you're going to play, even though you may have formed some first impressions.

Actress invited to play Beverly in *Abigail's Party*:
How old is she? And what do I think about her age?
She's five years younger than me, am I going to look mutton dressed as lamb? No, I haven't changed a bit in looks in that time.

Peasant in *The Caucasian Chalk Circle*:
How does he speak?
Well, it's Brecht, and they're peasants, but he says some very shrewd things, and so does his wife, and he's got a good vocab-

ulary. The director said we've got to make the characters recognisable. They live in the mountains, might they sound like fierce Kirk-going Scots?

Actress playing Raymonde in Feydeau's *Flea in Her Ear*:
How to convey a sense of the character's Frenchness?
The play's in English, so the attitudes, clothes, morals, temperament must be French, not the accent. I must read up on the life and habits of such a woman. What *does* she have in her handbag? I know, I'll ask the director if I can have a tiny thick posh diary, with a lock on it and a tiny fiddly gold key, oh, and she always wears gloves. I bet she takes them off last of all when she undresses: sexy hands!

Actor playing Sir Wilful Witwoud in *The Way of the World*:
Class – does it matter?
Yes it does. *The Way of the World* is all about snobbery and cash and superiority. But Sir Wilful Witwoud is an oaf and a drunken bum, and has a broad Shropshire accent. Aaah, you can be a rich country nob, and be totally thick, (educated by a wet clergyman, *they* went to university). Why's he always so drunk? Because it's so cold and boring there, that's why he didn't take his boots off before going in to dinner, he sleeps in them: NB ask director if I can have some huge, down at heel boots.

Characterisation is nearly always a mixture of things drawn from several human models and all these qualities must finally belong together, so reject those that don't fit. Rehearsal is the time for selection, for experiment and 'What if ...?' The free flow of ideas, memories and connections must be allowed to happen, and the actor must give himself time to explore. Sometimes a particularly strong image will trigger a characterisation. There is a tale of Olivier's famous tarantula-like Richard III, whose bizarre appearance and demeanour was supposed to be based on the Broadway director Jed Harris, with whom Olivier had worked. Harris was a notoriously despotic director and Olivier hadn't enjoyed the experience.

The experienced actor thinks simply but deeply, and tends to follow a few hunches. It has been the fashion in recent years to create a past and a future for the character the actor is playing, but whilst it's most useful to know how he or she became the person now to be brought to life, and to know their world, you can get bogged down in a lot of pseudo-psychological data. A dramatic character will not stand up to psychoanalysis; what's needed is a deep human understanding, and the profoundest common sense.

Opposites in character

As we have just seen, a characterisation is a putting-together of many qualities both physical and mental: appearance, age, health, energy, dress, habits, along with temperament, intelligence, attitudes, education, and likes and dislikes. One or two of these visible characteristics will be of paramount importance: a costume and the actor's bodily demeanour can convey dramatic meaning most vividly, so too can a prevailing attitude or emotion. Hedda Gabler's principal emotion is intolerable boredom, a weary, restless sarcasm and hardly concealed despair that such a feeling produces.

In compiling the 'blueprint' of a character it is vitally important to look for the opposites and paradoxes in all human beings. To illustrate this point, let us look briefly at the characters in *Othello*. Iago would be a very one-note character were he played only for his scheming malignity, his coarseness and cruelty. He is Othello's long-standing friend and colleague, indeed an intimate friend and confidant, and undoubtedly a fine, brave and effective soldier. He should be played as a man of ease, authority, persuasiveness and bonhomie, good company in the bloodiest fight, equally good company in the tavern, and capable of being at ease with men of all ranks, from the private soldier to the general. Othello is a very superior man, intelligent, resourceful and noble, who would not be duped by someone of obvious villainy. It's Iago's tragedy too, and we should watch aghast at the schemings of this funny, daring and attractive man, as he destroys others and finally himself. The actress playing Desdemona has the opposite problem – how to give Desdemona some spunk and show that Othello hasn't run off with a Venetian Barbie doll: so the actress playing her should search the text for the signs that reveal a warm-hearted sexy flirt, but capable of loyalty, sympathy and passion.

To play the opposite sides in any character of any reasonable dramatic size is to create electricity and tension *within* the character and to make them a rounded human being.

Working a Scene

Back to Olivier, perhaps because he was the actor par excellence: he said that he would sooner work through a scene eight times rather than discuss it. There often *is* need for discussion, to share wisdom and feelings, a sense of mutual exploration, but this must not turn rehearsal into a talking-shop. You must follow the great director John Huston's advice to his daughter Anjelica when stuck: 'Just *do it*, honey.' Relationships evolve and assume meaning by actors speaking to each other, touching or not touching each other, reading each other's body and vocal signals. Even a solo speech alone on a stage is usually speaking about a relationship of some sort. So at least three things have to emerge as the actors work together. First, the characters' attitudes and feelings toward each other. Next, their spatial and tactile relationship; it's perfectly possible to play a scene of love and tenderness while standing up several feet away from each other, and to play a scene of detestation whilst sat side by side on a small sofa. Lastly, and integral with the first two, a vocal sense, a musical pattern will became evident. The actors are exchanging words, giving and receiving, making an ensemble of different sounds that has some of the quality of music. From *Rosencrantz and Guildenstern are Dead*, by Tom Stoppard:

ROS	Heads.
GUIL	(*flipping another coin*): Though it can be done by luck alone.
ROS	Heads.
GUIL	If that's the word I'm after.
ROS	(*raises his head at Guil*): Seventy-six love. (*Guil gets up but has nowhere to go. He spins another coin over his shoulder without looking at it, his attention being directed at his environment or lack of it.*)
ROS	Heads.
GUIL	A weaker man might be moved to re-examine his faith, if in nothing else at least in the law of probability. (*He slips a coin over his shoulder as he goes to look upstage.*)
ROS	Heads.
	(*Guil, examining the confines of the stage, dips over two more coins. As he does so one by one, Ros announces each of them as 'heads'.*)
GUIL	(*musing*): The law of probability, it has been oddly asserted, is something to do with the proposition that if six monkeys (*he has surprised himself*) ... if six monkeys were ...
ROS	Game?
GUIL	Were they?
ROS	Are you?
GUIL	(*understanding*): Game. (*Flips a coin.*) The law of averages, if I have got this right, means that if six monkeys were thrown up in the air for long enough they would land on their tails about as often as they would land on their –
ROS	Heads. (*He picks up the coin.*)

A most delicate, musical and surreal conversation between two bored and polished men, which demonstrates a particular forte of Stoppard's: people talking about thinking. The comic sub-text is that Rosencrantz guesses wrong every time, so working the scene requires an actor to discover how to time his reactions to his extraordinary bad luck. For a man who's just lost the toss of a coin eighty times in succession he is remarkably hopeful and surprisingly unbitter. A rhythm emerges in that Guildenstern always allows him a pause to examine the coin and to react to the fact that it's always tails. The play is a delicate conceit about two celebrated fictitious nonentities, whether they exist or no, do they only exist in other people's minds – and we should have the feeling as they speak that they might in a moment be obliterated by silence or overtaken by an echo. However, a scene like this must be worked again and again, since it needs immaculate timing and great skill in carrying out the coin business. One dropped coin and the scene is ruined.

Timing

Rehearsal is when the timing and pacing of the play and the acting from moment to moment is established, both of which are the key to communicating with the audience. The prime example of timing and pace is the act of the stand-up comedian, whom we can describe as a solo actor, telling the audience about the drama of his life, the people he meets, the misfortunes that usually befall him (remember the actor's function as storyteller, as explored in the invented sci-fi narrative in Chapter 2, (p. 17). Let's look at a passage of text to see what precise quality of timing is needed to make it work for the watchers and listeners. This extract is from *A Flea in her Ear* by the master of farce, Georges Feydeau. Raymonde and Lucienne, two charming wives of a certain age, are discussing whether or not Raymonde's husband, Victor-Emmanuel Chandebise, has taken a mistress, to account for a falling-off in his performance of conjugal duties:

RAYMONDE	Oh yes? What about *that*, then? (*She takes a pair of braces from her bag.*)
LUCIENNE	What about it?
RAYMONDE	A pair of braces.
LUCIENNE	I can see that.
RAYMONDE	And who do you think they belong to?
LUCIENNE	Your husband, I assume.

RAYMONDE	You admit it!
LUCIENNE	Not exactly. I just presume that if you have a pair of braces about you they belong to your husband, *and no one else*!
RAYMONDE	Precisely! And now perhaps you can explain why he got them this morning, through the post.
LUCIENNE	Through the post?
RAYMONDE	In a parcel which I opened by mistake, when I went through his letters.
LUCIENNE	Why go through his letters?
RAYMONDE	To see what's in them.
LUCIENNE	Sound reason...
RAYMONDE	Well!
LUCIENNE	So that's what you call a parcel 'opened by mistake'?
RAYMONDE	Of course it was a mistake. It wasn't meant for me.
LUCIENNE	I see...
RAYMONDE	You agree that if someone posts him his braces, it's because he left them behind in some – *somewhere*?
LUCIENNE	(*Rising and moving down stage*) It seems to follow.
RAYMONDE	(*Moving down to her.*) Yes – and do you know where it was? This 'somewhere'?
LUCIENNE	You're making my flesh creep.
RAYMONDE	'The Hotel Coq d'Or', my darling.
LUCIENNE	What on earth's that?
RAYMONDE	Well, it's not the Christian Science Reading Room.

This little scene contains several of the basic ingredients of playing comedy, surprise, paradox, timing and an excellent verbal gag. Raymonde is in charge of the surprises and Lucienne acts the role of the surprised 'feed'. The paradox is that two elegant women are having a perfectly serious discussion about an intimate and suggestive item of menswear, and the braces themselves, produced with a flourish like a rabbit from a hat, take on a bawdy life of their own. The second paradox is in the way Raymonde thinks; she believes it entirely correct that a wife should sift through her husband's mail. 'Precisely' is the key to Raymonde's playing of the scene. She is rapid and neat of speech, because she has *already* found her husband guilty. So she must fire off a series of statements and questions which catch Lucienne off-balance; Lucienne responds with what I can only describe as fast dithering; her timing is dictated by the fact that she is struggling to keep up with the speed of Raymonde's thoughts. Raymonde's attack is clean and quick and throughout she is slightly increasing the pace before getting to the punchline, and Lucienne's attack often starts with a small pause. The actresses and the director should try to anticipate where the laughs are going to come, though this can never be firmly determined till the scene has been played before several audiences. Raymonde states the obvious by saying 'A pair of braces' with tart disapproval, which should produce a chuckle, and Lucienne's follow up 'I can see that' can also get a laugh if thrown away in mock alarm. The enchanting Geraldine McEwan, in a celebrated production at the National Theatre, made Raymonde even funnier by investing her with a plummy swooping contralto voice capable of every innuendo. The quick-fire exchange can only be created in rehearsal, but the scene is utterly dependent on the agility of the timing, and Raymonde is also controlling the speed of the audience's reactions.

The timing of a performance and the timing of a scene between actors is already implicit in a well-written text, but is capable of adjustment. If you are asked to play a scene or part of it more quickly, don't respond by rushing the words; speak them with greater agility, but find a reason for a quicker pace in the character and text. For example, the actress might think: I'll heighten the mood, she's more *impatient* than I'm playing her, more excited or crosser. Similarly, when asked to slow down the tempo, handle this by appearing to choose the words used with greater care, finding obstacles and diffi-culties in a character's understanding. The scene we've just looked at is capable of such adjustments: Raymonde can fizz with indignation and over-rule Lucille; or Lucille can fail to comprehend exactly what Raymonde is getting at. Raymonde may dramatise the situation she imagines she's in, feeling self-pity and betrayal as well as indignation and suspicion.

Listening and reacting

The timing of a scene will only emerge if the actors are listening to each other with the greatest concentration. Acting is action and reaction, and one of the most valuable actors is he or she who can play in a long scene where he's got little to say and a lot to listen to. It's wise to write your own sub-text, a scenario of your part in the scene – how you are affected, influenced or changed by what the other characters say, and how much physical and facial reaction is called for. This should always be economical, true to both character and situation. Over-reacting, unless it has a dramatic reason, destroys credibility, though it is a device often used in comedy as an expression of disbelief. The very major part of reaction is achieved simply by listening.

Pacing Rehearsal

If the actor is to be comfortable and creative during rehearsal he must pace himself and his work with fellow actors. The director will have a tentative plan of his objectives: when he thinks the play should be taking on a physical shape, when relationships should be clearly established, when the narrative element in the play should be clear. This is only a tentative plan, and director and actor must trust each other, since the entire process of rehearsal may be one of growing understanding, exercising very difficult skills, balancing intentions against obstacles and finding ways of expressing character. One of the most profitable things the actor can do is to learn the words before the half-way point in the rehearsal process, learning them without positive commitment to their meaning, which will be discovered during the exploratory process. Forgetting the text momentarily suspends character and narrative. Older actors in particular should make an early start on learning, as age makes memorising lines harder, and all actors should find time in rehearsal to take notes of any useful and important points that arise. Some find it useful to write out a paraphrase of a scene's content, the character's intentions, situation and progression of emotion. Learning lines is the actor's basic chore and it's sensible to learn moves at the same time, to gain physical freedom as soon as possible. Difficult business with props, dancing, fights must be worked at from an early stage of rehearsal. Don't lay down your script till you are reasonably sure of the lines, as someone being prompted every other line is tiresome for the entire company. Long speeches in particular need early examination; how much do they advance the action of the play? How do they deepen our understanding of the character? What reaction does the speech produce in the other characters? What is the climactic point of the speech or the most important thing said? This mini-drama is the actor's equivalent of an aria, and must be examined for its variety of tempo and note, after some discussion with the director.

Final Rehearsals

Two-thirds of the way through rehearsal the facts should be known and the objectives in sight. This is the time for development and consolidation, and major changes of interpretation, character and stage business should not be undertaken unless vitally necessary, as they will disconcert the other actors. Not that rehearsal can always be a smooth progression since actors work at different speeds, some parts are easier to understand and play than others, and many performances don't take off till the final run-throughs. It is at this point that the actor and actress really need to trust themselves, their fellow actors, the director and the team. But especially themselves, because at this stage the rather magical things I spoke of in Chapter 1 begin to happen, unbidden by the actors. Perhaps playing comedy is a more conscious process as it is so very technical relying on timing, pacing, accuracy and alertness. Good final rehearsals are the product of all the hard work by the actors throughout the whole rehearsal process. If a sound technical structure has been constructed, many things will flow easily and almost automatically, the sign of well-rehearsed actors. But remember, what has been a two-part relationship, between actors, their helpers, the production team and the text, is about to become a triple alliance as the audience joins in. So the whole structure must have an elasticity and be capable still of fine adjustment of mood, timing and interplay. A small ripple of amusement may have the potential to turn into a big guffaw from the audience; a minute or two of quiet attention may become a scene of rivetted interest and tension. A play, especially a comedy, can only grow and develop with *performances*.

Getting on to the Stage

At last the play transfers from rehearsal room to stage. The stage will be a pretty chaotic place before dress rehearsal, with stage management and the technicians sorting out scenery, props, lighting and sound, but the actor must find time to acclimatise himself to the setting. In the rehearsal room it's usual for the stage manager to mark out the set or sets on the floor, exactly the same size as they will be on the stage, but imaginary scenery is a very different thing from real doors, walls, windows and backings, so the actor must check everything he physically uses or touches, particularly doors. He must check the positions of property tables, and practise with the real props he's going to use on stage, as they will probably be different from the rehearsal props in size and weight, and all 'business' must be meticulously rehearsed before dress rehearsal. Furniture, especially sitting furniture will feel different from the usual hard chairs of the rehearsal room, so practise all 'sits'. Check the amount of time it takes to get from the dressing room to the stage, the position of anything stored in the wings, and the means of getting from one side of the stage to the other. The stage and backstage are now your workroom, so you must know the area intimately for your own comfort and security. Make sure you know all movements of scenery, trucks, flying pieces, in fact anything that moves, as the stage can be a dangerous place.

Get used to the auditorium. The actor enters a dark void, but faces a fierce battery of lighting which can be disorientating. Some plays are very much behind the imaginary 'fourth wall', where the audience are onlookers; other plays invite much more contact with them, that is, with the audience almost a participating character. The actor must also check out the auditorium for sound levels, to determine how much voice to use. Bear in mind that a full house needs louder speech than an empty one, and that many tiny fifty-seat fringe venues need almost no projection and an almost conversational level of speech can be clearly heard.

An actor in the theatre has an obligation to arrive at the theatre on the 'half', that is, thirty-five minutes before the show starts, but any actor playing a demanding part should aim to arrive early, to get into costume, to apply a complicated make-up if it's called for, above all, to focus his or her mind on the play, the character, his fellow actors. To the actor in the theatre, his dressing room is a sanctuary where he can rest, prepare and concentrate, so sharing a dressing room needs tact and consideration.

All good actors have suffered from stage fright at some time or other. I have already looked at ways of dealing with it in Chapter 2. That most immaculate of elegant comedy actors, Rex Harrison, said that he endured it throughout his career, and many stars have had incapacitated periods when they could only work for the camera. Laurence Olivier and Ian Holm, two Masterly actors, both suffered long periods of this miserable affliction. Indeed, whilst some roles are easy to play, the actor can never be complacent, and a self-satisfied and conceited actor is probably a careless and sloppy actor. The buttresses against the actor's major affliction are: thorough and detailed preparation and research, never-ceasing searching for the highest technical skills; a proper balance between alertness and bodily and emotional relaxation, and last, the knowledge that the audience very probably admires the actor for his or her courage, for transporting them into a world of imagination and understanding.

Performance

The actor must act what he and his fellows have rehearsed. When a performance 'takes off' it is due to excitement, a sense of occasion, the thorough and meticulous rehearsal which gives the actors a sense of security. Objectives are known, the psychology and humanity of the play is deeply bedded in the actors' minds, and their technique is being used to the full: timing, pacing, meaning, vocal variety, agility of interplay, reactiveness, expressive movement and body language. Collectively, the actors are telling a story, and living it out, spontaneously, originally, *in the moment*. The great imponderable is the people it's for, the audience. Their excitement, their interest must be engaged so that an invisible current, an unspoken understanding flows between them and the actors, a special kind of tryst. *Every* performance in the run of a play is as important as the first, and freshness, a sense of wonder, must be sustained; this is much easier to do when the actor has his technical skill at his fingertips – it will see him through when he's got an overdraft, a divorce or a pain in the belly. Things go wrong, and every actor has a few hilarious stories of stage disasters. Crises must be dealt with calmly, even if it means walking off the stage to collect the missing property. Bear in mind that the audience may often not know the play and be unaware of what will happen or be said next. It might be prudent to prepare one or two ad-libs in the manner of the play, though most experienced actors can usually cope by taking the dialogue back or ad-libbing appropriately, even playing other actor's lines for them!

Taking a prompt

The greatest actors sometimes need a prompt. An occasional 'dry' is not a catastrophe, merely a momentary hiccup. I suspect the audience sometimes enjoy these shows of human fallibility from actors. When you dry, don't snap your fingers, don't gaze in desperation at the prompt corner, or call out 'prompt'. Wait, don't lose your cool, and *listen*. Prompts should be given clearly, and it's the actor's business not to break the mood of the scene, but to get on with it as if nothing untoward had happened. Pick up the scene, with focus and concentration and if one of your fellow actors has come to your rescue, be sure to shower him or her with grateful thanks later.

In bringing your performance to the stage or before the cameras, there is one sole aim, perfection. That perfection can only be based on the highest technical skill, used resourcefully, flexibly and with a love for the audience. Good acting is not an ego-trip, it's an act of honesty, love and generosity.

7
Acting Shakespeare

Shakespeare is the most-performed dramatist of all time. He wrote thirty-seven plays between 1584 and 1613, which are acted world-wide in many languages, and have been televised and filmed. Scholars, commentators and critics continually write about, analyse and discuss them.

The reason for this is that they are wonderful plays, of profound humanity, intelligence and beauty of language. The thematic ideas that inform most of them are timeless, and the human psychology they examine is that of all humanity; after four hundred years they are still relevant to our modern world. Let's just list a few of these central ideas:

Measure for Measure Great men's abuse of authority. Man as a toy of lust. The valuing of chastity above life, the moral dilemma.

Love's Labour's Lost Exquisite comic romance. The immaturity of young men compared with women, and the need to love truly and simply and honestly. Intellectual pretension.

The Merchant of Venice Racial and religious bigotry and intolerance, anti-Semitism. Money the God in a mercantile society.

King Richard the Third A country trembles under a cruel and ruthless despot. The lust for power.

Timon of Athens Does money buy true friendship?

King Lear Parenthood. Old age. Deception and fatal misjudgement. Ingratitude. Duty to parents. Power, what makes it possible, and the relinquishment of power.

Romeo and Juliet The magic of first love and sexual passion. Marriage as a means of consolidating or raising family status in a rich bour-geois society. Feuding and fighting, the cheapness of life, wasteful and tragic death.

Shakespeare wrote about most aspects of human life and created a vast gallery of brilliantly drawn people, which is why actors, directors and designers come back to him again and again. He was a typical Renaissance artist, of that time when man threw off the narrow

The author's production of **Love's Labour's Lost** *with students of LAMDA's post-graduate course.*

scholasticism and chilly, tortured spirituality of the Middle Ages, and became free to celebrate or mourn the realities of earthly existence, in body and soul. Man also rediscovered the world of Greece and Rome, its art and culture, and even more importantly he rediscovered that he could think and reason. In the plays Shakespeare is describing the flowering of humankind and human intellect through discovery, politics, science, art. This new enlightened thinking brought about a reassessment of beliefs and a subtler understanding of human weakness, cruelty, vice, greed and folly. The only significant theme not examined by the plays is the Church and all its works, though God and the gods, oracles, priests, witchcraft and the supernatural are frequently evoked.

The Form and Structure of the Plays

Acting Shakespeare is the actor's greatest challenge. It is axiomatic to say that if you can act Shakespeare you can act anything. Like any other great dramatist Shakespeare needs fine and truthful acting, and a wide range of expressive techniques, especially vocal expression. The largest part of the language of the plays, some seventy-five percent, is in verse, the rest in prose. This verse is in a form known as the iambic pentameter: it's not in rhymes and couplets, but contains basically ten syllables to the line, five of which are stressed, the other five unstressed. This is known as 'blank verse', and goes like this:

de dum de dum de dum de dum de dum

Director John Barton says that this rhythmic form approximates more closely than any other poetic metre to everyday speech in English, so it's not the straightjacket it might seem to be. We'll examine the purpose and use of these speech forms later in the chapter.

Modern practice, since the innovative director William Poel early this century, has been for designers and directors to create a 'machine to act in', rather like Shakespeare's theatre, that is, a simple and atmospheric box or space which can be changed, diminished or enlarged according to the needs of the scene: actors might be seated on two stools, tightly lit with the rest of the stage in darkness, or the back wall of the acting area might fly out to let a battle, a procession or a pageant take place. Costumes may be wittily updated, or bear a resemblance to the locale and period of the play. The 'Roman' plays, for example, are usually acted in Roman dress, the toga and Roman military wear. The things that we invariably dispense with are realistic scenery, properties and furniture. So already there's a hint that the actor, his body and body-language are what we're supposed to be looking at, rather than scenery. This implies that the plays are very rich in physicality and action. There are a lot of characters in each play who interact strongly with each other: Othello with Iago and Desdemona, Iago with Roderigo and Cassio and Emilia, Emilia with Desdemona, Iago and Othello, to take examples from just one play. The plays were originally written in a five act form with many scenes. Those scenes and divisions, contrasts and juxtapositions still exist, though we tend now to tailor the play into two halves and make it move rapidly. In the days of Henry Irving and Herbert Beerbohm Tree vast quantities of artistic and real-looking scenery were thought to enrich the experience, but it took an awful lot of time to change from scene to scene, and to us today would seem to impose the wrong kind of naturalism on a production. All the plays contain long speeches, some of which are soliloquies, that is, where the actor is talking to himself or herself, or thinking aloud when alone. Language is generally used at greater length, more profoundly and richly than in the modern play, and is seldom as colloquial and chatty; so the repeatedly lifted inflections of contemporary speech aren't used nearly so frequently. It can be seen that acting Shakespeare is the very converse in almost every way from acting in television or films. Yet as drama they are organically related: the same truth and personation and expression, but conveyed with a very different technique.

When we set about acting Shakespeare, we have to reconcile two different acting traditions, modern, easily spoken naturalism with its life-like and conversational quality, which appears to require no effort to speak, and Shakespeare's vivid image-laden language, with its obvious rhythmic form. The Shakespearian acting of our time is of high quality, because of the technical skill and the modern actor's sense of realism. We must also acknowledge his use of formal and ceremonious behaviour, the behaviour of great people in royal courts. All the plays contain grand setpiece scenes of this kind, where 'natural' behaviour in our modern casual sense would under-mine the dramatic effect of great intensity created by the use of heightened language. I said in Chapter 1 that some late 18th and 19th century actors used the texts for virtuoso displays of bombastic oratory and showy swaggering, and often rewrote and manipulated the text to provide for sentimental endings; it seems that they couldn't bear the playwright's truthful rigour. The actors who created these characters in Shakespeare's time worked under pressures that no contemporary actor could cope with, and rehearsal was incredibly brief, a day or two at most, yet the audience went away satisfied. How did they do it? They were the everyday, realistic actors of their time, and they studied the text in a way we all should do, for just below the surface are many stage directions: where to move, how close, how long to hold a pause, is she smiling or stoney-faced? Patrick Tucker, who is both director and scholar, recently gave an impressive demonstration that this *could* be done and produce good results. The actors were given 'cue scripts,' on fabric scrolls; these contained only that particular actors lines, and in every case the few words preceding his utterances. The actors, who were all playing parts in plays with which they were unfamiliar, went away and overnight learned their speeches, and cues for speech and action. They were then thrown straight into rehearsal, or rather performance, and immediately the scenes took shape. A salutary lesson in how to read a scene for its sub-text, the action *implicit* in *the lines* rather than appearing on the surface.

Present-day Shakespeare

A modern audience, who are exposed to a great diversity of good acting on the screen, want their Shakespeare to be understandable and life-like; so the actor is moving fluently between verse and prose, smooth, slightly underplayed speech, and heightened speech. Hamlet's advice to the players is the most famous short crash-course in acting, all acting, including the modern play, and after four hundred years as trenchant and wise as ever. It deserves selective quotation and must be a constituent of any observations on acting anything, let alone Shakespeare. It's in prose:

> Speak the speech, I pray you, as I pronounced it to you, trippingly on the tongue. But if you mouth it, as many of our players do, I had as lief the town crier spoke my lines. Nor do not saw the air too much with your hand, thus. But use all gently. For the very torrent, tempest, and, as I may say, whirlwind of your passion, you must acquire and beget a temperance that may give it smoothness...
>
> Be not too tame neither. But let your own discretion be your tutor. Suit the action to the word, the word to the action, with this special observance, that you o'erstep not the modesty of nature...
>
> For anything so o'erdone is from the purpose of playing, whose end, both at the first and now, was and is to hold, as 'twere, the mirror up to nature.

The contemporary English-speaking actor seems to be doing his best to follow these injunctions, and avoids posturing, orotundity and mannered speech and movement. The ideas in Shakespeare's dialogue are very well expounded, and it's the ideas and thinking of the characters that must come across. Periodicity is less important, and the modern actor is in fact acting the plays more naturally than was the case in preceding centuries.

Speech and Language, Verse and Prose

By 'heightened language' we mean language rich in imagery, metaphor and simile, language which is evocative, where the exactly right words are used to create the maximum depth of understanding and feeling. Blank verse is the most common form of language used by the Elizabethan and Jacobean playwrights, so the actor must learn to make proper use of it and enjoy it. It seems to be so effective as a means of communication because it's so easy to listen to. I said that the prevailing verse pattern was of alternate stresses over ten syllables, thus: de dum de dum de dum de dum de dum. Were this to be an absolutely regular rhythm, the audience would be rapidly lulled into boredom or sleep. Let's look at a speech which is in verse, and replete with images and rich description. It is from *Antony and Cleopatra*, where the tough soldier Enobarbus is describing Cleopatra's river-borne first appearance to Agrippa:

> I will tell you.
> The barge she sat in, like a burnish'd throne,
> Burn'd on the water: The poop was beaten gold;
> Purple the sails, and so perfumed, that
> The winds were love-sick with them; the oars were silver,
> Which to the tune of flutes kept stroke, and made
> The water which they beat to follow faster,
> As amorous of their strokes. For her own person,
> It beggar'd all description. She did lie
> In her pavilion, cloth-of-gold, of tissue,
> O'er-picturing that Venus, where we see
> The fancy outwork nature. On each side her
> Stood pretty dimpled boys, like smiling Cupids,
> With divers-colour'd fans, whose wind did seem
> To glow the delicate cheeks which they did cool,
> And what they undid, did.
> ...Her gentlewomen, like the Nereides,
> So many mermaids, tended her i' th' eyes,
> And made their bends adornings: at the helm
> A seeming mermaid steers: the silken tackle
> Swell with the touches of those flower-soft hands,
> That yarely frame the office. From the barge
> A strange invisible perfume hits the sense
> Of the adjacent wharfs. The city cast
> Her people out upon her; and Antony,
> Enthron'd i' the market-place, did sit alone,

> Whistling to the air; which, but for vacancy,
> Had gone to gaze on Cleopatra too,
> And made a gap in nature.

This magnificent speech presents many of the problems inherent in speaking Shakespeare and needs careful examination. It incorporates archaic words and phrases:

> The silken tackle
> Swell with the touches of those flower-soft hands
> That yarely frame the office.

We must translate; it means that the sails billow as a result of the maiden's soft hands that speedily and efficiently do their work as sailors! A delightful notion: the men presumably are out of sight, pulling like hell on the oars. Having satisfied ourselves that we know what we are talking about, we must use Shakespeare's language exactly, to the last syllable. We are using a language which is unique in its beauty and richness, and expresses the writer's thoughts and meanings exactly. To alter it in any way would be heresy.

The actors of Shakespeare's time, however, didn't speak modern southern English R.P. as described in Chapter 3. It hadn't even evolved, and their accent was more like that of the present day educated and articulate American, an accent that has its roots in the west-country speech of the founding fathers of the United States. It is a moot point whether Americans acting Shakespeare should not do so in their own accent, rather than working for a polished British R.P.

Let's start taking the speech to pieces, examining its form and meaning. First and foremost, it's a 'choric' speech, a narrative of action and a description of people, things and events, not apparently a speech about the speaker, his situation and feelings. Yet it reveals Enobarbus as a man not only of wonderful powers of observation (the senior soldier), but a man of sophistication and culture; also as a romantic sensualist who can revel in the beauty and magnificence of what he's seen. We don't expect a burly soldier to be bowled over, and his appreciation of the experience is a most interesting facet to his character, revealing unexpected depths. It ends with a fine bit of humour, with the image of a rather grand Antony, doing the heavy pro-consul and having his dignity and importance severely dented, an example of a piece of characterisation emerging from what another character says about him – a momentary image of a testy Antony looking a considerable fool.

Mood and pace

Look at the vowel sounds in the first four lines, and they will give you an indication of the tempo of the speech, a recollection is being savoured:

> The b<u>a</u>rge she sat in, l<u>i</u>ke a b<u>ur</u>nish'd thr<u>o</u>ne,
> B<u>ur</u>n'd on the w<u>a</u>ter. The p<u>oo</u>p was b<u>ea</u>ten g<u>o</u>ld;
> P<u>ur</u>ple the s<u>ai</u>ls, and s<u>o</u> perf<u>u</u>méd that
> The winds w<u>e</u>re love-sick with th<u>e</u>m: the <u>oars</u>...

A lot of long vowel sounds, which I've underlined, should have their full sonority. By this, I don't mean that the lines are in any way 'intoned', but they should be spoken thoughtfully and with relish; to describe this speech I'd say he was 'speaking long'. Examine the vowel sounds and they usually give a feeling of the overall tempo and when it changes. The punctuation as in modern dialogue has an effect on pace (I use pace and tempo interchangeably); here, in four lines we have a full stop, a colon, a semi-colon and three commas. Enobarbus is reflecting and choosing what are for him exactly the right words to describe what he saw. I've put an acute accent over the -ed ending of 'perfumed', to show that it needs to be pronounced, to give the right number of syllables, which is known as 'syllabifying'. Note that 'burnish'd' has an apostrophe instead of an 'e' to show that you *don't* syllabify. The basic rule is, use it if it makes sense and gives the line ten syllables. Not that all the lines have this regular rhythm: modern acting demands that you inflect, that is stress for sense and emotional meaning. But an exaggerated naturalism, with supplementary noises and pauses, makes nonsense of the style of language:

> The ... ah ... oars were ... er ... silver,
> Which to the toon of er ... flutes kept ... ah ...
> stroke ...

Another device brought into play here is onomatopoeia, that is, words which have something of the effect of what they are describing: 'tune of flutes' has a musical quality, 'kept stroke' a crisp, metronomic sound, providing in two phrases a contrast in sound. Alliteration is also used: 'follow faster', 'many Mermaids'. You can see that this speech goes far beyond mere talk or conversation, yet it must sound like natural speech.

Shaping a speech

A long speech has a shape, a profile: imagine this speech drawn as a graph, and think that it is rising to a peak of interest and excitement. In speaking blank verse, with its linguistic richness, inflection and

122

Michael Bryant as Enobarbus in the Royal National Theatre's production of **Antony and Cleopatra.**

stress must be subtly used, and quite long passages can be spoken with little change of note: think of the effect of music, which makes frequent use of repeated notes. This speech seems to fall into four sections. The first describes the barge itself, the second, beginning 'For her own person....' as far as Agrippa's interruption subtly arouses interest in Cleopatra by *not* describing her, but depicting her attendants and the sumptuous pavilion she lies in, the magnificent barge, and the whole exotic ambience. The speech contains much reference to rhythmic movement, the beat of the oars synchronised to the music of flutes, so the words in a way mirror the surging advance of the barge, drawing closer. Perhaps the pace and volume are increasing slightly, hence the excitement. The third part of the speech is hypnotically vibrant, with Cleopatra's women described as sea-nymphs (Nereides) and mermaids 'At the helm, a seeming mermaid steers'. Calmly, with contained excitement, Enobarbus is describing an experience so beautiful and remarkable as to seem like a dream or an illusion. His excitement can only show through the vibrancy of his tone. Now we come to the climax of the speech.

From the barge
A strange invisible perfume *hits the sense*
Of the adjacent wharfs.

Cleopatra is described as a magical emanation; the words 'A strange ... invisible ... perfume' are said slowly, and it's the only part of the speech that actually describes her. A pause, then the excitement bursts through:

The city cast her people out upon her!
(I've added the exclamation mark)

He rounds up the speech with a fine comic flourish, with Enobarbus being rhetorical, amused and ironic in his description of Antony's discomfiture. The last two lines are said slowly, with a warm humour, and again, there is a sense of command in what he's saying:

... th'air; which, but for vacancy,
Had gone to gaze on Cleopatra too,
And made ... a gap ... in nature.

Here I've tried to show the beats that could be used in the last line: the effect is rather like a huge and glittering car coming to a halt; the brakes must be heard to go on, rather than the speech ending abruptly or merely tailing off. Enobarbus tells a good story.

As can be seen, the speech is sometimes irregular in the number of stresses each line contains, and sense must take precedence over regular and rhythmic stressing. Some eminent Shakespearean actors vary widely in the way they use the stresses. This speech illustrates how vividly a character emerges out from Shakespeare's use of language. Enobarbus is a man very much like Antony, of similar age, occupation, culture and intelligence, but very different; he is able to observe Cleopatra with delight, but not enslavement – at the last, a self-serving and above all detached man.

Shakespeare's Prose

Prose has no fixed rhythms, as does the pentameter, but has rhythms of its own. Here is an example from *Macbeth*:

PORTER	Faith, sir, we were carousing till the second cock; and drink, sir, is a great provoker of three things.
MACDUFF	What three things does drink especially provoke?
PORTER	Marry sir, nose-painting, sleep, and urine. Lechery, sir, it provokes and unprovokes: it provokes the desire, but it takes away the performance ...

This scene is preceded by:

LADY MACBETH	... A little water clears us of this deed. How easy is it then! Your constancy Hath left you unattended. (*Knock*) Hark! Get on your nightgown, lest occasion call us, And show us to be watchers. Be not lost So poorly in your thoughts.
MACBETH	To know my deed, 'twere best not know myself. Wake Duncan with thy knocking! I would thou could'st!

This is a remarkable transition from highly-charged verse to fine sardonic prose. There are no rules about when the dramatist uses verse and when prose. Shakespeare seems to make the switch when he feels it to be right, so we must try to get a clearer idea of the contrast between the scenes, and look at their differences in tone.

Macbeth is a complex tragic figure, a good man corrupted by ambition. A nobleman, a confidant and friend of the King of Scotland, a victorious general, he is subjected to temptation by the appearance of the witches, agents of the supernatural, perhaps the devil, certainly the forces of darkness, who have the power to intervene in human life. They tell him he will become King. Lady Macbeth is even more complex; ruthlessly ambitious for Macbeth, eloquent, powerfully seductive, possessed of a ghastly courage, she sets humanity and conscience aside in the pursuit of earthly prizes, urges her husband on to regicide, and thereafter is pursued by her Nemesis: the torments of a guilty conscience and fear of everlasting perdition. Two formidable figures, mature but not old, for whom sexual passion is the cement of their marriage. Macbeth has the wider view of human life, and his pain springs from his reflectiveness, his philosophical intelligence.

Macbeth has murdered Duncan, and Lady Macbeth has planted the bloody daggers on the king's groomsmen, drunk and sleeping in his chamber, and smeared their faces with his blood. Macbeth is freezing with horror and guilt:

Methought I heard a voice cry
'Sleep no more;
Macbeth does murder sleep' ...

and

'... Macbeth shall sleep no more'.

She is more resolute, and has her wits about her:

Why did you bring these daggers from the place?
They must lie there ...

It is a scene which cries out for verse, and gets it: Macbeth again

Will all great Neptune's ocean wash this blood
Clean from my hand? No, this my hand will rather
The multitudinous seas incarnadine,
Making the green one red.

She is all action:

... retire we to our chamber. A little water clears us of this deed.

The murder is a dream-like nocturne with its nightmare atmosphere, intense speech, two darting, bloodied figures seen by torchlight. With the porter's salty prose cold reality dawns, and we re-enter the real world of normal people, whose worst crimes are to drink too much, acquire red noses, and commit laughable sexual indiscretions. The porter's observations are in the same vein of wisdom as those of Alfred Doolittle, discussed in Chapter 3, and whilst being an amusing character, he's also serious. The prose used in this little scene is also a relief from the unbearable tension of the preceding one. It is, too, an opportunity to 'reculer pour mieux sauter': for the scene that follows is also highly dramatic, showing the grief and horror of Macduff and Lennox, the terror and suspicion of Malcolm and Donalbain that they might be next for the chop, and the masterly performances of woe and grief given by the murderers.

In a very short scene the porter speaks some fine muscular prose, and juggles with antitheses most eloquently. Antithesis occurs again and again in Shakespeare's dialogue; in brief, it is the contrast of words and ideas, the notion that every effect or action must have an opposite, in meaning, act, place or feeling.

So what appears to be a jocose if sharp speech by a 'funny' character turns out to be a neat and well-thought digest on the subject of equivocation, that is, hedging, white lies, double meaning, ambiguity, uncertainty; paradox – an almanack of antithesis:

Here's a farmer that *hang'd* himself on the *expectation of plenty* ...
Faith, here's an *English* tailor come hither [to Hell] for stealing from a
French hose [stocking] ...
Lechery sir, it provokes and unprovokes ...
It makes him and it mars him ...
Makes him stand to, and not stand to ...

The porter's prose is highly memorable, and all men will wince slightly
at his precise definition of that distressing affliction known as Brewer's
Droop. Shakespeare's modernity is always surprising, and often funny.
Prose is not used only for minor characters, funny characters or the
lower orders. The famous 'sleepwalking' scene from the same play is
almost entirely in prose, only turning to verse in the doctor's last
speech. It is a celebrated scene because of its intense dramatic quality
and most especially its psychological truth and insight. It's so real it's
as though we were hearing the confessions of a murderess who has
been injected with a truth-drug; it has strange staccato rhythms
which 'ambush' us, and the scene is utterly unpredictable. Let's look
at some of it:

> *Enter Lady Macbeth, with a taper.*
>
> GENTLEWOMAN Lo you, here she comes! This is her very guise; and,
> upon my life, fast asleep. Observe her; stand close.
>
> DOCTOR How came she by that light?
>
> GENTLEWOMAN Why, it stood by her. She has light by her continually;
> 'tis her command.
>
> DOCTOR You see her eyes are open.
>
> GENTLEWOMAN Aye, but their sense is shut.

A rapid, whispered or low-voiced conversation, broken by pauses
while they observe her.

> DOCTOR What is it she does now? Look how she rubs her hands.
>
> GENTLEWOMAN It is an accustomed action with her, to seem thus wash-
> ing her hands; I have known her continue in this a
> quarter of an hour.
>
> LADY MACBETH Yet here's a spot.

If this is timed right, and acted right, it has the same blood-curdling
effect as a bloody hand reaching up from a grave:

> DOCTOR Hark, she speaks. I will set down what comes from her,
> to satisfy my remembrance the more strongly.
>
> LADY MACBETH Out, damned spot! Out, I say! One, two; Hell is murky.
> Fie, my lord, fie! A soldier, and afeared? What need we

> fear who knows it, when none can call our pow'r to
> account? Yet who would have thought the old man to
> have had so much blood in him?

A chillingly strange speech by a woman in an altered state, talking to herself, or rather to the Macbeth present in her dream, reliving yet again the awful emotions of that moment, repeating those actions like a wind-up doll. Her speech is low and intense, but no longer business-like and calm; guilt and fear have added a tremor to her voice. She is a woman on the edge of an abyss.

DOCTOR Do you mark that?
LADY MACBETH The Thane of Fife had a wife; Where is she now? What, will these hands ne'er be clean?

The last line is a low, despairing wail. We hear that her dream is not a consistent experience – as in a nightmare, things blur and start before her 'eyes'.

> No more o' that, my lord, no more o' that; you mar all
> with this starting.

This last rapid and staccato. The doctor is appalled by the depths of Lady Macbeth's infamy and by the danger it represents to the fabric of the state and society. And only learned, close, discreet people like doctors can share great and dreadful secrets, not women who are mere attendants:

DOCTOR Go to, go to; you have known what you should not.
GENTLEWOMAN She has spoke what she should not, I am sure of that. Heaven knows what she has known.
LADY MACBETH Here's the smell of the blood still. All the perfumes of Arabia will not sweeten this little hand. Oh, oh, oh!
DOCTOR What a sigh is there! The heart is sorely charg'd.
GENTLEWOMAN I would not have such a heart in my bosom for the dignity of the whole body.

The doctor is reduced to complete perplexity, he's never seen such a condition.

DOCTOR Well, well, well.
GENTLEWOMAN Pray God it be, sir.

The last two lines are another good example of the dramatic effect of antithesis and irony – 'Pray god it be, sir.' Tart and ironic, it has the power to startle us. Acting, not just in Shakespeare or in comedy where it's a principal ingredient, is about surprise, which is what I meant when I said that the scene ambushes us. The more or less regular rhythms of verse would destroy this scene's dramatic qualities, so it's another example of the playwright choosing exactly the right medium for the scene.

The scene ends with verse, after the exit of Lady Macbeth.

DOCTOR	Will she go now to bed?
GENTLEWOMAN	Directly.
DOCTOR	Foul whisperings are abroad.
	Unnatural deeds
	Do breed unnatural troubles; infected minds
	To their deaf pillows will discharge their secrets.
	More needs she the divine than the physician.
	God, God forgive us all. Look after her;
	Remove from her the means of all annoyance,
	And keep still eyes upon her. So, goodnight.
	My mind she has mated, and amaz'd my sight.
	I think, but dare not speak.
GENTLEWOMAN	Goodnight, good doctor.

'Mated' in this context means bewildered, derived presumably from checkmated. The return to verse is a return to the formal mode which drives the play along and seems a good medium for the doctor's slightly sententious conclusions. Indeed, such couplets to end a scene are known as 'sententiae'.

To sum up, Shakespeare's prose needs meticulous speaking; its innate rhythms must be discovered, for in them lies the mood and tempo of the scene. As in all Shakespeare, speaking the lines leads to their acquiring meaning, so do it again and again, to allow meaning, pace, rhythm, to float to the surface. Whilst it's very necessary to have a clear idea of their content and to know the meaning of archaic words and grammatical constructions, what the actor is seeking is the truthful expression of the text.

Character

Whilst the verse form is easy, musical and seductive to listen to, at times Shakespeare's characters can tend to sound somewhat alike. What is the difference between Bushy, Bagot and Green (*Richard II*), who sound like three sneaks out of a school story? Or the multitude of knights, peers and grandees who people the Histories in particular? Or the comparative individuality of either Rosalind or Viola? In the early and splendid days of the Royal Shakespeare Company, the three parts of King Henry VI and King Richard III were artfully cut and edited together to make a trilogy under the omnibus title of 'The Wars of the Roses'. Give or take a few, this meant some thirty-five noblemen, excluding kings, queens, duchesses, French nobles, arch-bishops, mayors and so on. Critic Ken Tynan, in one of his inspired moods, said that a short speech to characterise the confusion of this exalted pecking-order would go: 'Surrey! I am thy cousin's brother's eldest son!'

Miraculously, we understood exactly where everyone stood in this huge game of Realpolitik: how much power they had, where they lived, north or south, *what they wanted*, what strength of character might help them achieve their ends, what weakness would lead to their downfall. In the preparation of this production the directors were influenced by the Polish scholar Jan Kott, who in his book *Shakespeare our Contemporary* looked at the way power changes hands according to the personalities of those wielding it, seeking it or abdicating from it. The actors made these shadowy characters exist in the here and now by applying the same methods of creating a character in Shakespeare's text as we have discussed in previous chapters, as they would to a character by Shaw or Arthur Miller. That is, to discover their intentions and wants (motivations) and to find out as much of their character as is revealed in the text, their relationships with others, their wealth, status, temper, what others say about them. You may not find much of this information in smaller characters, so the actor has to make a set of likely conjectures, backed up by his own research and understanding of the style of the production. The dukes and noblemen in the Histories are more realistic social and political figures than Orsino in *Twelfth Night*, or Prospero, exiled Duke of Milan in *The Tempest*. Indeed, all Shakespeare's characters must be endowed with their own reality, even supernatural or fantastic characters like Ariel, described as 'an airy spirit', in *The Tempest*, and Oberon and Titania in *A Midsummer Night's Dream*, who are king and queen of the fairies. These characters present problems for the actors, the director and the designer, since their physical appearance is of the utmost importance. The theme running through most approaches to these characters is physical lightness and super-agility, and a striking quality of appearance. Oberon and Titania are characters of powerful sexuality, so their costumes must allow them to move freely and sensuously. There is an apocryphal tale of the actor-dancer Robert Helpmann and Vivien Leigh playing these characters in very elaborate costumes with ornate and complicated headpieces; on first greeting each other, these 'horns' became interlocked, and the quarrelling pair had an undignified wrestling match to part themselves, to the mirth of the audience. The actor Patrick Stewart, now Captain Picard of *Star Trek* acting Oberon for the RSC played him for modern ideas of male sex-appeal: lithe, bare-chested, long tangled hair, the wild man of the woods. There is a celebrated painting by the insane artist Richard Dadd (1858) showing a 19th century concept of these characters: Oberon is a bearded Middle-Eastern warlord, a gigantic heavy figure holding a spear – impressive, but no fairy. Titania is a mature matron of opulent figure, wearing an absurd crown and also carrying a spear. From her hairstyle, she appears to be a transmogrification of Queen Victoria.

So stage one for these two extraordinary creatures is to create a physical reality for them. Stage two, when working through the text and blocking, is to create a hyper-energy of movement and being. This doesn't mean they are frantically active or perform bizarre and mysterious actions, rather that they have tremendous presence, elegance, 'class'. Their agility and fluidity of movement should suggest that they might just vanish in a puff of smoke or flash of lighting. A modern audience, living in a scientific world of communications, politics and products responds eagerly to intimations that there is some ancient magic. Their text, though, is quite different from the mysterious premise of what they are – fairies. They are Kramer v. Kramer. All the ingredients of a marriage in disaster are there, in a thoroughly modern way: quarrelling over the custody of a child, accusations of infidelity, jealousy, mockery of rivals, threats of cruelty, pettiness, manipulativeness. This would be awful to witness if it were not apparent that this is a clash between two immense egos and, as a view of marriage, has an acid comic quality very reminiscent of the movies of Woody Allen. The play neatly draws the distinction between being in love, being smitten or having the hots (Titania by magic is deluded into a violent fancy for a man turned donkey) and real love. It's a comedy about love, a cautionary tale.

The text provides the clues to the downright humanity of the fairies; it's a delicate juggle between their supernatural qualities and the fact that they behave just like that couple we know:

OBERON   Ill met by moonlight, proud Titania.

Not the most conciliatory approach to a wife you're rowing with. Titania can give as good as she gets:

TITANIA   What, jealous Oberon! Fairies, skip hence: I have forsworn his bed and company.

Let the neighbours know! She adds with a sneer:

> When thou hast stolen away from fairy land, and in the
> shape of Corin sat all day, playing on pipes of corn, and
> versing love to amorous Phyllida...

So the fairy king chats up other women, dressed as a shepherd, and
plays them little tunes; what fools husbands make of themselves! The
dispute about custody of the boy is not resolved:

OBERON   Give me that boy and I will go with thee.
TITANIA   Not for thy fairy kingdom. Fairies, away ...

Oberon is furious:

> Well, go thy way; thou shalt not from this grove
> Till I torment thee for this injury.

He summons his magic minion Puck, and calls for a special herb, to
be squeezed into Titania's eyes:

> The next thing then she waking looks upon,
> Be it on lion, bear or wolf or bull,
> Or meddling monkey, or on busy ape,
> She shall pursue it with the soul of love ...

This would be a monstrously cruel trick if we took it too seriously, but
we know that at the wave of a magic wand all will be well again.
Oberon should be charming and confident, his tongue slightly in his
cheek, as it's also like a schoolboy's gleeful prankishness.

Titania wakes and the first thing she sees is Bottom, the weaver,
transformed; by magic he has an ass's head, which talks, winks, leers
and brays. Anthropomorphism in reverse. The tradition is still alive
and kicking, that is, the attribution of human characteristics,
personality and behaviour to animals – see Mickey Mouse, Donald
Duck, Goofy and Garfield. It seems to serve as a reminder that we too
are animals, and in spite of our power to reason shouldn't get above
ourselves. It's also a badge of the fearfulness and cruelty of nature (the
dreadful Duke Ferdinand in Webster's *Duchess of Malfi* in his final madness imagines himself to be a wolf, except that his skin is hairy on the
inside). That Bottom is turned into half an ass is poetic justice, because
he *is* an ass in the other sense, a likeable but boastful chatterbox, bossy
and overwhelmingly self-centred. The ass is also a grossly sexual
animal, a coarse beast of all work. This would again be cruel and
deeply uncomfortable if Titania hadn't got it coming to her. In spite of
her supernatural powers, like her husband she is flawed, hugely vain,
capricious, affected and often silly – they are spoilt rich kids. Yet at the
same time she's adorable. Perhaps the key theme of the play is not

magic, which is a mere device, but the notion that sexuality, lust, is an awful power, that can cloud our judgement, obliterate our common sense, and wreck our loyalties. So we'd better see the funny side of it.

The egregious Bottom, shunned by his mates, utterly unaware that he is physically changed, says:

> I see their knavery: this is to make an ass of me; to fright me, if they could ...

He sings a little song (surely a naughty song about phalluses?), to keep up his spirits:

> The ousel cock, so black of hue,
> With orange-tawny bill,
> The throstle with his note so true,
> The wren with little quill.

He is at best a robustly voiced bar-room singer, but his vocal talents are not improved by his partial metamorphosis: donkey noises keep on creeping in, snorts and ee-aws. We must feel that if he had a brother in the animal kingdom it would be a donkey just like this. An amiable raucous fool. Titania wakes. After a huge double-take and a quivering indrawn breath, she goes into her flirtatious and adulatory mode, batting her eyelashes:

> What angel wakes me from my flow'ry bed?

and:

> Mine ear is much enamoured of thy note;
> So is mine eye enthralled to thy shape; ...
> And thy fair virtue's force perforce doth move me,
> On the first view, to say, to swear, I love thee.

Note the alternation of verse and prose; different rhythms are part of characterisation. Bottom unknowingly is in a different physical world and body, Titania in a different world of emotion, perception and meaning. Bottom gives her a little bar-room wisdom:

> Methinks, mistress, you should have little reason for that.
> And yet, to say the truth, reason and love keep little company together now-a-days ...

The funniest and most foolish character in the play captures its essence and deepest meaning.

Titania's subsequent behaviour is the key to her character. She is not a woman who's been brain-washed by a drug into completely uncharacteristic behaviour; her predatory, voluptuous flirtatiousness was always there, the gush, the dramatic behaviour. She's simply letting it hang out, and has lost all her inhibitions, the posh lady being a roaring sexpot. She's funny because of her passion for so incongruous a lover; the avidity of her feelings for him is reflected in the breathy quiver in her voice as she offers him celestial treats and comforts:

> I'll give thee fairies to attend on thee;
> And they shall fetch thee Jewels from the deep,
> And sing, while thou on presséd flowers dost sleep ...

And

> Feed him with apricocks and dewberries,
> With purple grapes, green figs, and mulberries;
> The honey-bags steal from the humble bees ...

All to the end of:

> Come, wait upon him; lead him to my bower ...
> Come, sit thee down upon this flow'ry, bed
> While I thy amiable cheeks do coy,
> And stick musk-roses in thy sleek smooth head,
> and kiss thy fair large ears, my' gentle joy ...

She gives him the full comic-seductress treatment, and he responds with the feelings that are at the heart of his character, immense, stolid complacency:

> Scratch my head, Peasblossom ...
> I had rather have a handful or two of dried peas. But,
> I pray you, let none of your people stir me;
> I have an exposition of sleep come upon me ...

The scene, with its exaggerated emotion from Titania, and the smug, uncomprehending self-satisfaction of Bottom, could in its emotional and mental content come from a very superior modern sit-com – indeed, this situation and these characters have probably reappeared in many a script.

What has emerged from a brief examination of this scene is that Shakespeare's most fantastic characters, indeed all his characters, only develop and take on their strong identity if we look for their *humanity*: vices, faults, virtues, intelligence, sense, humour, morality. They are not types or abstractions, but real people, however fantastic their occupation or situation may be: to be a fairy king is simply a profession; to have an ass's head is to have a most embarrassing rash, or to wear catastrophically inappropriate clothing.

Language and accent

A further important aspect of characterisation is *accent*. *A Midsummer Night's Dream* has three distinct groups of people, who must be differentiated by the way they speak. There are the royal and aristocratic Athenians, Theseus and Hippolita, Egeus and the four young lovers; the rustic artisans, 'rude mechanicals' of whom Bottom is the self-elected leader; and the fairies, Oberon, Titania, Puck and Titania's attendant fairies. Clearly the royals and gentry speak very good R.P. or whatever accent is appropriate, the mechanicals must have a degree of unity in their accent to indicate more their class than their origin. In British productions this is usually southern English peasant speech of a vague and general kind, often referred to as 'stage Mummerset', but there's no reason why they should not speak in any English or American country accent, as long as they can be clearly understood. The one accent that doesn't work is any sort of big city accent, Cockney, Scouse, New Yorker. They are essentially country folk. The fairies are best off spoken in R.P.; certainly their speech must somehow capture the same energy and perhaps slight strangeness that their movement suggests. Puck, a curious androgynous creature who is equally well acted by a man or a woman, is above all, a very clever *child*, sexless, mischievous and sometimes very sad. He croons, sings, parodies, puts on funny voices; a protean display that must make us wonder just what he is. He is utterly alone, a brave and mysterious little creature.

The effectiveness of accent has been demonstrated by the remarkable Ian McKellen, playing Richard III. His performances are always distinguished by precision and ingenuity of characterisation. His Richard is a smooth, pallid, slightly deformed electric eel, but the most striking characteristic is his use of an extraordinary 'advanced R.P.', an aristocratic accent of the greatest individuality, eccentricity and arrogance. By this means, he conveyed the impression that he was the only true aristocrat present, that he was the possessor of royal mysteries and strange knowledge, that he was superior in every way to those around him – a daring technical device, superbly carried off by a virtuoso actor.

Shakespeare and the Classical Repertoire

Acting what is known as 'the classical repertoire' is the crown of acting in English. By this term we mean a whole body of plays which have passed the test of time. Over decades and centuries these plays have been successfully revived because of their humanity, depth of insight, humour, feeling and pungency of observation. The best of modern plays eventually join this body of work for the same reasons. Great plays by writers from other countries, translated into English, are also part of the classical repertoire: Molière, Racine, Schiller, Ibsen, Chekhov. I've dwelt on Shakespeare because he is the finest of a group of remarkable Elizabethan and Jacobean poetic dramatists, whose work is of a similar kind. Kyd, Jonson, Marlowe, Webster and Tourneur are the greatest of them, and the same approach and techniques need to be applied when acting them. There is also a body of Elizabethan bourgeois comedy, known as 'City comedies' which deals with the emergent mercantile middle and lower-middle classes. They are mainly in prose. After the Restoration, language changed and prose became the instrument, though there is an innately poetic quality in the language of Congreve, for example, which often has exquisite beauty and rhythm. From *The Way of The World*:

MRS MILLAMANT One no more owes one's beauty to a lover, than one's wit to an echo. They can but reflect what we look and say; vain empty things if we are silent or unseen, and want a being.

MIRABELL Yet to those two vain empty things you owe the two greatest pleasures of your life.

MRS MILLAMANT How so?

MIRABELL To your lover you owe the pleasure of hearing yourself praised; and to an echo the pleasure of hearing yourselves talk.

WITWOUD But I know a lady that loves talking so incessantly, she won't give an echo fair play; she has that everlasting rotation of tongue, that an echo must wait till she dies, before it can catch her last words ...

Witty and delightful conversation, and enchanting vocal music.

Shakespeare, however, remains at the heart of the classical repertoire, for the sheer number of his plays, their variety and magnificence. Let's try to summarise the core skills needed to play him

1 A big breath capacity, smoothly and easily handled. Mastery of the 'snatched' breath, and the ability and energy to 'attack' again and again in the course of playing a big part. (Rosalind, Hamlet, King Lear, Cleopatra, for example). Control of 'intensity'.

2 Great relaxation of the vocal equipment, so that there's *always* a good quality of tone. The voice must be well placed to project; Shakespeare is usually played in big theatres, and the actor mustn't shout.

3 A good range of notes, and the musical and rhythmic sense to use them subtly – even conversations are less chattily inflected than in modern telly sitcoms.

4 Agile, muscular articulation, tireless tongue and lips. Shakespeare and his contemporaries set the actor endless tongue twisters. Sit near the stage, and you'll see even the finest actors spitting over the orchestra pit!

5 Bodily energy, fluidity and agility. The imagination to explore movement possibilities; you are the focus of visual interest, not your clothes or the scenery.

6 Bodily repose; being still for long periods without losing energy or presence. Fidgeting ruins Shakespeare's language and thought.

7 Exploration of character and the ability to make his characters human, even fairies, sprites and ghosts.

8 An enjoyment of the beauty of the language. Enjoy also the modernity, truth and profundity of his ideas, and his humour, which is always around, even in the tragedies.

8
Looking at the Whole Play:

A Streetcar Named Desire

We need now to examine a play as a whole, to analyse the text, get a picture of the plot and action, try to feel the quality of the language, and most importantly, form a good idea of the characters, their relationships with each other and the world at large. This is how a director might work with a cast of actors in pursuit of the what, where, why and how. I've chosen a celebrated and important modern American play, because the previous textual examples have largely been English. This play looms large for consideration in depth because it is in many ways the archetypal American play, by America's greatest dramatist. There are other American play-wrights with high claims to greatness: Williams's contemporary Arthur Miller, Eugene O'Neill, the innovatory, beguiling and neglected Thornton Wilder, Edward Albee, and the prolific master-craftsman, Neil Simon. But Williams has something very special which raises him above the others: an audacity in writing about the torments of the human heart, a vision of the look, scent and touch of life and the world, and a genius for poetic language, both exquis-itely tender and hauntingly savage. Whilst he wrote in prose, he must be considered a 'poetic' dramatist because of the music and imagery of his dialogue:

> But a poet's vocation, which used to be my vocation, is to influence the heart in a gentler fashion ... He ought to purify it and lift it above its ordinary level. For what is the heart but a sort of – a sort of – *instrument*! – that translates *noise* into *music*, chaos into – order ... a *mysterious order*! – That was my vocation, once upon a time, before it was obscured by vulgar plaudits! – Little by little it was lost among gondolas and palazzos! – masked balls, glittering salons, huge shad-owy courts and torch-lit entrances! Baroque facades, canopies and carpets, candelabra and gold plate among snowy damask, ladies with throats as slender as flower stems, bending and breathing toward me their fragrant breath –
>
> (Lord Byron, from *Camino Real*)

Into the mouth of Byron, Williams has put his own intent and passion. From the accounts of his friends he was a merry, melancholic sybarite, a witty talker with a huge laugh; a homosexual who devoured the pleasures of the flesh, drink, drugs, food, men, places, company, things, atmospheres. His immensely superior sensibility and intelligence raised him above mere passions of the body, and whilst homosexual in his preferences, he knew, loved and understood women. Probably the greatest love of his life, along with his friend and lover Frank Merlo, was his sister Rose – a fragile drifting creature from the age of thirty, who at the behest of his mother suffered a lobotomy, and for the next forty-two a years lived in a twilight world, incapable, gentle, cared-for.

She is the model for the crippled Laura in *The Glass Menagerie*; in the same play the genteel tyrant Amanda Wingfield is modelled on Edwina, the author's mother. Miss Rose can be found in a whole gallery of Williams' tragic women who are lonely victims: Alma Winemiller, and Blanche Dubois, even partly in Hannah Jelkes in *The Night of the Iguana*, Williams's last great play. Hannah is realistic and resolute, but homeless in middle age, dependent on what she can hustle by painting and sketching strangers, and accompanied only by her senile grandfather, whose very presence precludes any other intimate relationships: she, like Miss Rose, is chaste. The theme of woman in peril is taken to the point of extreme danger in *Suddenly Last Summer*. Kathy Holly knows how her rich playboy cousin, the debauched pederast Sebastian Venable has met his death; he has been pursued by a horde of exploited boys, his intended sexual prey, and torn to pieces – the starving kids have *eaten* large parts of his body. '*They had devoured him...*' says Kathy, under the influence of the truth drug. Sebastian's harpy-like mother, the rich socialite Mrs Venable, has determined to suppress the sordid truth of her son's awful life and death, which can only be done by conspiring to have Kathy lobotomised at the sinister mental hospital, Lion's View. Her cruel scheme is thwarted by young Dr Kukrowitz: Kathy is given Pentothal, and the horrible truth emerges at the end of the play, in an immense and dramatic speech, like an avalanche of the emotions. The play has the horror and grandeur of Euripides, grasping the great issues of hubris, life and death. It is Williams' revenge for the hacking in two of Miss Rose's poor brain. In play after play, he confronts the extremities of the human condition: loneliness, alienation from others, inordinate sexual passion, disease of the body and disease of the mind, poverty and desperation. His plays are peopled with fugitives, on the run or gasping in some temporary limbo, probably reflecting his own flight from a cruel father, a snobbish mother, and stiff old-fashioned society. In a world where there are so many women victims, there are likely to be male oppressors and Williams is sensitive to the fact that America, that still young Utopia, is a man's world. In *Streetcar* Blanche Dubois is a kind of victim; Stanley Kowalski a kind of oppressor. All this would seem to give a picture of Williams as a very gloomy dramatist, a Southern Strindberg, but he isn't. His plays are incandescent with lights and harmonies, moments of joy, humour and irony. He's writing about the real world, and the longed-for perfect world, the phantasmagoria seen by so many of his characters. He writes tenderly about the people of the melting-pot that is America, where the old is in constant conflict with the new, where 'class' as a definition of status is melting away in the face of modern industrial prosperity, equality and democracy. Personal history is very important to Williams, as it is to Arthur Miller. The past must be recalled, be relived, if it is to be evaluated or exorcised, a dramatic method also used by Chekhov. Williams declared to Dotson Rader, his biographer, that Chekhov was the major influence on his writing and this should remind us that Williams is above all a naturalistic writer, however heightened the language and situation.

Streetcar, the Play

Streetcar is a tragedy. It's the tragedy of Blanche Dubois, who because of her heritage, her beliefs and her frailties, because of her history, succumbs to madness: she can't cope with the realities of money (the need to be self-sufficient), with emotional truths. Blanche is a thirty-ish Southern belle, and the comforts and foundations of her life have slipped away; the family estate and fortune have gone due to her profligacy and the way the times have changed. She is snobbish, arch, old-fashioned, egotistic and a drunk. She is also cultivated, refined, artistic, often witty, elegant and beautiful. And desperately lonely. Desperately insecure; she has nobody to share love with. She too is in flight, and winds up on the doorstep of her sister Stella in a sleazy quarter of New Orleans. Stella, who is twenty-five, is married to Stanley Kowalski, a working man, grandson of Polish immigrants, a man who's triumphantly proved his manhood in World War II: he was a master-sergeant and a war hero. A life-force, a complete American, his name could be chiselled on the Statue of Liberty. Stanley is uncouth: he works, eats, drinks, bowls, plays poker and copulates with Stella with uncomplicated avidity. He doesn't spare anyone; he's a man meeting modern life and struggle head-on. One line in the second act sums up this savage and ruthless side of him: his buddy Mitch is weeping with rage and reproof as the medics take Blanche away to the asylum – Mitch too is lonely, and has fallen for Blanche:

MITCH   (*wildly*) You! You done this, all o' your God damn interfer-
         ing with things you -
STANLEY Quit the blubber! (*He pushes him aside.*)
MITCH   I'll kill you! (*He lunges and strikes at Stanley.*)
STANLEY *Hold this bone-headed cry-baby*! [my italics]

Williams was a consummate man of the theatre, and all his plays have a rich visual quality, of setting, furnishing, costuming and locale. He knew exactly how he wanted it to *look*, and as a 'poetic realist', how the transitions of mood and atmosphere from scene to scene were to be effected. In his descriptions of his characters, we're reading about people who have been deeply, understandingly observed. Accents must be exactly right, which is where the expert dialogue coach must be called in to help. The play is set in New Orleans, but contains a subtle diversity of Southern accents. Blanche is a lady, a schoolteacher of English and literature, and a woman of considerable social pretensions; speech and language to her are an assertion of status. Stella is also a lady, an educated woman, who has moved down socially. Yet she lives easily with her husband and her neighbours, so much of the ladylike mode of speech has been happily discarded. Recognisably sisters, they are yet very different in that Stella invariably talks warm wholesome common sense, whilst Blanche is always 'performing'. This very disparity of speech is a major factor of her character – what's she hiding?

Our image of Stanley and his sound will be forever haunted by the memory of Brando, who played him in the 1950s Elia Kazan stage production and film, but woe betide any other actor alive who tries to imitate him. Brando is unique, and this was one of his greatest performances. Stanley talks from necessity, and to him only a fool wastes words; he says in Scene 1 'I never was a very good English student'.

Here is an exchange between Stanley and Blanche in Scene 2. This is the opening round of a contest to the death.

STANLEY I don't go in for that stuff.
BLANCHE What – stuff? [Note the tiny, angling pause.]
STANLEY Compliments to women about their looks. I never met a
         woman that didn't know if she was good-looking or not
         without being told, and some of them give themselves
         credit for more than they've got...

and:

STANLEY	Some men are took in by this Hollywood glamour stuff and some men are not.
BLANCHE	I'm sure you belong in the second category.
STANLEY	That's – right.
BLANCHE	You're simple, straightforward and honest, a bit on the primitive side I should think. To interest you a woman would have to – (*She pauses with an indefinite gesture.*)
STANLEY	(*SIowly*) Lay ... her cards on the table. [A shrewd and accurate assessment by Blanche. Maybe she can't cope with men, but she can read them – an indication of the recent course of her life, for better or for worse, she knows what to *do* with them.]
BLANCHE	(*Smiling*) Yes – yes – cards on the table ... Well, life is too full of evasions and ambiguities, I think. I like an artist who paints in strong, bold colours, primary colours ...

Williams describes his characters, as Shaw does, both their appearance and the impression they make:

BLANCHE Her expression is one of shocked disbelief. Her appearance is incongruous to this setting. She is daintily dressed in a white suit with a fluffy bodice, necklace and earrings of pearl, white gloves and hat, looking as if she were arriving at a summer tea or cocktail party in the garden district [The elegant quarter of New Orleans.] She is above five years older than Stella. Her delicate beauty must avoid a strong light. There is something about her uncertain manner, as well as her white clothes, *that suggests a moth.* [My italics.]

The last sentence is very helpful to the actress playing Blanche. It suggests a quality of pretty, hapless flutter and vulnerability, that she is a creature of the night. As indeed she has been.

STANLEY He is of medium height, about five feet eight or nine, and strongly, compactly built. Animal joy in his being is implicit in all his movements and attitudes. Since earliest manhood the centre of his life has been pleasure with women, the giving and taking of it ... with the power and pride of a richly feathered male bird among hens. Branching out from this complete and satisfying centre are all the auxiliary channels of his life, such as his heartiness with men, his appreciation of rough humour, his love of good food and drink and games, his car, his radio, everything that is his, that bears his emblem of the gaudy seed-bearer. He sizes women up at a glance, with sexual classifications, crude images flashing into his mind and determining the way he smiles at them.

A simple but powerful man, without sensitivity or subtlety, but street-wise, nobody's fool. Blanche has come to stay for an indefinite period and the tiny apartment becomes a pressure-cooker in which these two vastly different people will attract and conflict.

The Dramatic Action and Characters

The play is an unfurling of the personal history of Blanche, and charts the miserable few months before her descent into madness. She arrives on the Kowalski's doorstep in May of some year in the late 1940s, 1947 perhaps: World War II is not long over. They live in a small ground floor appartment of a two-storey frame house in the exotic poor quarter of New Orleans, where blacks and whites rub along together, so there's always music from the bar on the corner, called 'blue piano'. In the stage directions, music and sound are used throughout the play to heighten the atmosphere; the house is near the railway tracks, and trains roar past with blazing headlamps, like terrible monsters. The 'Varsouviana' a polka tune which Blanche associates with the long-ago suicide of her young husband is heard playing, in varying moods; we can hear it, but it's playing only in Blanche's head.

The central dramatic action is the fierce conflict and growing hatred between Blanche and Stanley. Stanley is an unwelcoming host and Blanche a jittery, tippling, sharp-tongued guest. They are both figures of powerful sexuality, so desire is never far from the surface. Stanley suspects Blanche of having dissipated the Dubois family fortune; in a horrid scene which foreshadows the eventual rape, he tears open her trunk and scatters her clothes, furs and jewels, thinking that they are her ill-gotten gains from the great house, Belle Reve, now lost to Blanche and Stella. So in his mind, Blanche stands condemned of having defrauded his wife of her inheritance. He sets out to discover all that has happened in Blanche's recent past, and Blanche lies, fabricates and fantasises to support the fictitious picture she has painted of herself. She also tries to undermine her sister's marriage to 'an animal'. These scenes are interspersed with ominous scenes of violence – a drunken Stanley beats up Stella, but she's deep in sexual thrall to him, pregnant, and despite the coarseness, the brutality, she's happy with him. More and more floats to the surface about Blanche's past: a long string of casual lovers and protectors, a shameful end to her teaching career (she had seduced a seventeen year old pupil). Blanche has now set her cap at Mitch, Stanley's workmate and ex-army buddy. Mitch seems different: a dutiful son to his ailing mother, a good-mannered gentle giant, a gauche and innocent man. These two lonely people draw closer to each other. At intervals Blanche becomes more honest. She confesses to Stella:

> That's why I've been – not so aw'fly good lately. I've run for protection, Stella, from under one leaky roof to another leaky roof – because it was storm – all storm, and I was caught in the centre ... People don't see you – *men* don't – don't even admit your existence unless they are making love to you. And you've got to have your existence admitted by someone, if you're going to have someone's protection...

She tells Mitch the painful story of her teenage marriage to an artistic boy, how she discovered him in a room with a man, having sex. Her young husband then shot himself. Blanche is slipping. She makes a pass at a young man who calls at the house. Blanche and Mitch have a date; she resolves to play the lady who doesn't 'put it about', so that Mitch will desire her the more. Before that relationship can go any further, Stanley tells Mitch all the sad details of Blanche's past, and Mitch cruelly rejects her. She is now sliding further and further into drunken fantasy and lies. Stanley takes Stella to the hospital to have her baby. On his return, drunk and celebrating, he finds a drunken Blanche, dressed in tatty finery, packing her clothes; she pretends that she has been invited by an old beau to go on a cruise. Stanley persecutes her unrelentingly. He provokes her to fury and terror, then rapes her.

Some weeks later, the medics come to take Blanche to the asylum. Stella says to her neighbour Eunice Hubbel, 'I couldn't believe her story and go on living with Stanley'. Stanley and his buddies are playing poker and drinking. The doctor gently leads Blanche away, leaving Stella sobbing and wracked with grief for the sister she has seen destroyed. As she weeps, Stanley comforts her by putting his hand into her blouse and caressing her breasts.

The events of the play move with an inevitable momentum, but it's a drama, not a documentary case-history. Its dramatic power lies in the conflicts between the characters, and the conflicts they have with their own selves, and in the rich immediacy with which the world of New Orleans is conveyed. We must consider the four main characters, Blanche, Stanley, Stella and Mitch, and try to discover the problems of acting them.

Blanche Dubois

The most celebrated role of the 'Southern Belle' apart from Scarlett O'Hara, and a character of much greater depth and interest. Like Hedda Gabler, she is a difficult woman, and a challenge to the actress.

The play was written over fifty years ago, so Blanche to a modern audience may well seem a figure from a remote historic world. She does indeed represent the old world crumbling before the assault of the new, but there's nothing old-fashioned about her agonising dilemma. It's a situation that many women have confronted, and will go on confronting: their role in society, their sexuality, their opportunities to determine their own lives, and their relations with men in a male-run world.

I said that the play is Blanche's tragedy, and this highlights the effect the actress playing her must have on the audience. Despite her grievous faults, she must enlist our sympathies, and despite her infuriating behaviour we must feel a deep sense of loss, sadness and anger at her ultimate fate, feel that a beautiful and delicate life has been torn and wasted. The actress's first consideration must be to make Blanche a serious and worthwhile woman, capable of intellectual, aesthetic and even moral delicacy. Her manners, her attitudes, her language and way of comporting herself are the result of an upbringing, a conditioning, of the values of America's Old South. We must go back to the child and the girl. Stella, whose words and judgement we instinctively trust, says 'You don't know Blanche as a girl. Nobody, nobody was tender and trusting as she was. But people like you abused her, and forced her to change.' 'People like you.' She means men, and their lust and sexual opportunism. This might refer to the male ancestors and kindred of the family, as described by Blanche: '... Our improvident grand-fathers and father and uncles and brothers exchanged the land for their epic fornications...' Blanche is not a phoney. She's a liar, but out of expediency; she's a snob, if snobbery is the possession of a sense of social superiority and high expectations she is a poseuse, if the display of a set of accepted manners language and behaviour is posing. A most important aspect of her is her previous occupation as a teacher of the English language, literature and poetry; she believes in art and culture. So her quotations from Whitman and Poe are not mere cultural name dropping and one-upmanship. Whilst a lot of her behaviour is foolish, and a lot of her conversation affected, she is not a silly woman, and is capable of sharp humour. Stanley is suspiciously examining the vast quantity of papers relating to the loss of Belle Reve:

BLANCHE   Here all of them are, all papers! I hereby endow you with them! Take them, peruse them – commit them to memory, even! I think it's wonderfully fitting that Belle Reve should finally be this bunch of old papers in your big, capable hands! ...

STANLEY	I have a lawyer acquaintance who will study these out.
BLANCHE	Present them to him with a box of aspirin tablets.

We can derive from the text something of Blanche's attitude to money:

> Y'know how indifferent I am to money. I think of money in terms of what it does for you ... and: Don't, don't laugh at me, Stella! Please, please don't – I – I – want you to look at the contents of my purse! Here's what's in it! (*She snatches her purse open.*) Sixty-five measly cents in coin of the realm! ... Money just goes – it goes places ...

Blanche has been protected by privilege and has expected that family and men will ultimately provide. She describes the men of her family as 'Exchanging the land for their epic fornications'. She's a dreamer and has no sense of financial reality. She regards her salary as a school-mistress as a mere pittance: 'A teacher's salary is barely sufficient for her living expenses...' She has been brought up to be extravagant, and it's a comment on Southern upper class society as well as a weakness in herself, a weakness heightened to a perilous dimension. Money, to Blanche, is safety and protection, and her only observable extravagances are liquor and finery, probably cheap and tawdry finery at that.

Williams spent his life wrestling with liquor and draws a painfully truthful picture of someone sliding into alcoholism:

> She pours a half tumbler of whisky and tosses it down. She carefully replaces the bottle and washes out the tumbler at the sink...

The self-deceptions and lies: 'No, I rarely touch it...' and:

> I'm not accustomed to having more than one drink. Two is the limit – and *three*! (*She laughs.*) Tonight I had three.

She is trembling on the brink of danger: she seldom appears drunk, but is drinking enough for her behaviour to become imprudent, and motor disturbances are beginning to show – the glass and the cigarette sometimes tremble in her hand.

She is, in some ways, like a confused innocent walking into the arms of her enemies, yet at times a greedy self-indulgent sensualist. We have the powerful contrast between her professed delicacy and her confessed feelings of strong sexuality, as strong as Stella's. She says of Stanley:

> But the only way to live with such a man is to – go to bed with him!
> A man like that is someone to go out with – once – twice three times when the devil is in you.
> What such a man has to offer is animal force...

She flirts with Stanley, and despite much complaint about the lack of privacy appears before him in her underclothes and asks him to button her dress. Life has taught her to use her attractiveness, and like other characters in Williams's plays, to seek oblivion and assuagement of unhappiness in the depths of sexual passion. For Blanche, this proclivity is full of shame, and she talks primly in terms of Protestant upper-class sexual morality:

> ...You can't have forgotten that much of our bringing up, Stella, that you suppose any part of a gentleman's in his nature!

Blanche's dilemma is that she has failed in the market place – she has not been able to sell her sexuality for secure marriage, which is the expectation of a woman of her class. Williams again and again shows us people at the capricious mercy of romantic fantasy and the power of lust, and Blanche has early declared her membership of this sad sisterhood in her marriage to a beautiful young poet. She is, perhaps still fixed in emotional immaturity, still an expectant girl of sixteen. A lot of the explosive tension in Blanche is self-hatred. She hates herself for her sexual vulnerability, for a long sad course of self-indulgence, for her unconfessed extravagance and folly. She is terrified of age and the eventual loss of her beauty, and has turned these fears into extraordinary tics of behaviour: professing to be younger than Stella, abhorrence of clear or bright lights which might reveal the beginnings of a wrinkle or two, (fear of the light is the symbol of her flight from reality), an obsession with personal daintiness and hygiene. She takes baths continually, if necessary at half-past two in the morning. It's rather like Lady Macbeth's dreadful midnight hand-washing, as though these ritual ablutions could wash away the sins of the past. She is seldom seen behaving unselfconsciously, since her upbringing has taught her always to present herself in the best light, both literally and metaphorically. The effect of this is often impressive, but highly inappropriate for the circumstances into which life has led her. She is always overdressed, an orchid in a farmyard; her body language is elegant and dramatic, incongruous against the backdrop of the apartment, with its shabbiness, cheap furnishings and lack of pleasing ornaments. The naked light bulb epitomises the pitiless exposure to which she is subjected. Her attempt to present an image of beauty, elegance and decorum is constantly undermined by starts and twitches; she is jumpy, like a moth speared on a needle, illuminated by torchlight. Where is there to flee to? There is no suggestion of serenity about Blanche – she hasn't got Stella's principal resources, which are robustness and acceptance.

She's a woman who has utterly lost her way, who's doing things the wrong way – a woman to be pitied. So the actress playing her must establish the seriousness and emotional intensity of her – the sheer *need*. She must also counterbalance these characteristics with humour and charm, and perhaps endow Blanche with a winning or endearing smile, moments of great tenderness, moments of genuine warmth, so that we feel for the woman who is losing her grip on life. We must love her beyond the play-acting.

Stanley Kowalski

The Diabolus-ex-Machina who is the instrument of Blanche's destruction. Our final judgement must be that his actions are unpardonable. He, after all, has control of his life. He represents bigotry, inverted snobbery, gross values and cruelty, male machismo at its most fearsome. But he too is a creation of his own past. A 'Polack' – his very nationality makes him an object of contempt in Anglo-Saxon America, where Polish history and culture mean nothing. He has spent several years under fire, under bombs, building bridges, up to his waist in a Pacific swamp where the leeches try to squirm into his jungle boots. The world of peace owes a debt to him, since he was one of its defenders. But Stanley has no political beliefs, and his world is very small: first, his family, and his own domination over it. He is a Catholic patriarch, however much he may think himself to be a modern American citizen: 'Remember what Huey Long said – "Every Man is a King!" And I am the king around here, so don't forget it!' Next, the world of men, of male camaraderie, and male recreations: bowling, poker, drinking, fighting, joking. The jokes are misogynistic:

STEVE   And the old lady is on her way to Mass and she's late and there's a cop standin' in front of th' church an' she comes runnin' up an' says, 'Officer, is M'ass out yet?' He looks her over and says, 'No, Lady, but y'r hat's on crooked!' (*They give a hoarse bellow of laughter.*)

I've added the inverted comma in the word 'Mass' to make the joke understandable.

Stanley is a creature of nature. He is uncouth and seems to be making no attempts to better himself socially, to rise to Stella's level; rather, he is determined that she shall exist on his. We can assume that he works with the same ferocious energy that characterises all his actions, an energy, animal vitality, is the key to the man, plus bursts of good humour, good looks, a smile that could melt rocks, and a most *dangerous* sex-appeal. If he wasn't a trucker, he'd be a movie star. His narrow personal morality would seem to consist of being a hard worker, a man of his word, a good provider on the basic level, and a zealous lover of his wife. Women have a very limited but powerful role in his life: they exist for bed, board and to produce children. He is a man existing in the moment, in an orgy of his own senses, and this must show in acting him. No man pulls on a bottle of beer, a glass of whisky, a cigarette, with more lip-smacking relish. In his garish bowling shirt he preens himself, wearing it proudly like gorgeous plumage. He is hardly capable of calm and moderate speech, swinging between the flatly, growlingly laconic and bellows of laughter or rage.

The other side to his emotional nature is the baby. Having beaten Stella up, causing her to flee to her upstairs neighbour, he stands in the street and bellows for her return like a frantic and angry three year old: 'Stella! Stella, sweetheart! Stella! I want my baby down here. Stella, Stella!'

His occasional forays into more formal language border on the comic: examining Blanche's furs:

> Genuine fox fur-pieces, a half a mile long! ... I got an acquaintance who deals in this sort of merchandise. I'll have him in here to appraise it ...

Stanley is a monster of selfishness and insensitivity. The cruel rape of Blanche is the act of a man without heart or understanding, a man who respects nothing and values no one, who is driven by instinct, and substitutes sentimentality for love. But there is little calculation in his acts. He is a fiery creature of impulse, a primitive hunter breeder, as symbolised by the bloody package of meat he throws to Stella in the first scene.

For the actor playing Stanley, there are several pitfalls to be avoided. It's important not to caricature his sexuality. His swagger and virility are real; unlike Blanche, he is incapable of play-acting and posturing. His powerful masculinity is revealed by his energy, his temper, his capacity for work, sex, liquor, his hardness, his uncompromising speech, his growling voice, his total contempt for all niceties. He must not appear and sound inarticulate – he isn't a moron, and is entirely capable of expressing what he *wants* to express. Stanley is, finally a tragic figure whose needs and lusts will in the end overwhelm him; only so many of the struggles of life can be overcome by force, and he is unable to understand, empathise or compromise. It is most important to see him from his own point of view. He genuinely believes that Blanche has cheated Stella, and himself, and finds her a subversive influence in his little kingdom. He loathes her for what he believes to be her falsity, for the social manner that represents the class that oppresses him. He believes, somewhere at the back of his mind, that Blanche will take Stella from him, and fears Blanche for her sexuality, a woman who won't kow-tow and submit to him, a woman who possesses the weapon he most fears and distrusts – a brain – and who's prepared to use it to survive.

Stella

Twenty-five years old. The temperamental opposite to Blanche, gentle, calm, serene, she has made Stanley the centre of her life. She is a contented prisoner of passion. After the beating in Scene 3:

> The door upstairs opens again. Stella slips down the rickety stairs in her robe. Her eyes are glistening with tears and her hair loose about her throat and shoulders. They stare at each other. Then they come together with low animal moans. He falls to his knees on the steps and presses his face to her belly ... her eyes go blind with tenderness ...

From Scene 4:

> BLANCHE   But you've given in. And that isn't right, you're not old! You can get out.
>
> STELLA   (*slowly and emphatically*) I'm not in anything I want to get out of.

She left Belle Reve at the age of fifteen, to shift for herself in New Orleans, and has thrown off her social status. She has adjusted completely to her neighbours, to her housing and income, and in the main is blissfully content. She is happily pregnant, and her habitual expression is a smile: and:

> BLANCHE   ... yes, you're plump as a little partridge!

and:

> BLANCHE   Look how quiet you are, you're so peaceful. Look how you sit there with your little hands folded like a cherub in choir!
>
> STELLA   (*uncomfortably*) I never had anything like your energy, Blanche.
>
> BLANCHE   Well, I never had your beautiful self-control...

Stella is the element of stability and normality in the play. She is always Blanche's protector and treats her with loving tolerance, excusing her faults, and, most importantly, showing us that Blanche is a lovable woman. Yet Stella is too sensible for hero-worship. She has taken on the role of older sister to Blanche and supports her with unswerving loyalty, even when it means that she must clash with Stanley:

> STANLEY   ... A seventeen-year old boy – she'd gotten mixed up with!
>
> STELLA   This is making me – sick!

Stella carries much of the narrative of the play. She is a sympathetic, warm and conciliatory person but she can't avert the final tragedy; she must go to hospital to have her baby, leaving Blanche to Stanley's mercy. Throughout the play she has suffered without complaint, though even she has a great moment of fury, when Stanley tosses the precious radio out of the window: 'Drunk drunk – animal thing, you!' Life for Stella will never be the same again. In spite of her tolerance, her generosity and goodwill, Blanche is destroyed. The sister she loves has been raped by the man she adores. She will have to live with that knowledge for the rest of her life, no matter how strongly she may deny the truth. Her refusal to admit to Stanley's guilt contributes greatly to Blanche's madness, for Blanche is denied justice, recompense and comfort. Stella has sacrificed Blanche to save Stanley, and we must leave the play with very mixed feelings about her.

The actress playing Stella must capture all her qualities: her gentle and sunny disposition, her common sense and adaptability, and her considerable sexuality, which is as warm and comfortable as Blanche's is sharp, corrupt and spiky. She is a strong woman, physically and emotionally; her tragedy is that she's not strong enough to contain Stanley. A tragedy of a woman who loves too much.

Mitch

Harold Mitchell, always diminished to 'Mitch' is the fourth corner of the play, like Stella a representative of normality and decency. He's an ordinary working guy, a skilled man, who's probably gone as far in the world of work as he's ever going to, a man in his later twenties who runs with the male pack, yet lives with his widowed mother. A deeply conventional man, gentle and well-mannered, but timid and circumspect. His life is much affected by what he is physically, and he is intensely self-conscious of his appearance:

MITCH	I am ashamed of the way I perspire ...
	... A man with a heavy build has got to be careful what he puts on him so he doesn't look too clumsy ...
BLANCHE	You are not the delicate type. You have a massive bone-structure and a very imposing physique ...
MITCH	I weigh two hundred and seventy pounds and I'm six feet one and a half inches tall in my bare feet – without shoes on. And that is what I weigh stripped.
BLANCHE	Oh, my goodness me! It's awe-inspiring.
MITCH	(*embarrassed*): My weight is not a very interesting subject to talk about ...

He is the antithesis of Stanley, cumbersome where Stanley is agile, ponderous where Stanley is mercurial, cautious not reckless, slow and thoughtful of speech. He is in many ways innocent and childlike, and the actor playing him might pause to think of his homelife – a gloomy apartment, a sick and demanding mother, whose apron strings tie him up. He's easy meat for Blanche, who in her desperation sees him as a refuge:

BLANCHE	... I want to create – *joie de vivre*! I'm lighting a candle.
MITCH	(*heavily*): That's good.
BLANCHE	We are going to be very Bohemian. We are going to pretend we are sitting in a little artist's café on the Left Bank in Paris! (*She lights a candle stub and puts it in a bottle.*) Je Suis la Dame aux Camellias! Vous êtes – Armand! Understand French?
MITCH	(*heavily*) Naw. Naw, I –
BLANCHE	Voulez-vous coucher avec moi ce soir? Vous ne comprenez pas? Ah, quel dommage! ...

It's Blanche's flattery and attention that draws him into her web, and he cannot see that it is a relationship doomed from the start:

MITCH	(*drawing her slowly into his arms*) You need somebody. And I need somebody, too. Could it be – you and me, Blanche?

Mitch is a figure of tragedy *and* comedy. He is an inept and groping wooer:

MITCH	Just give me a slap when I get out of bounds.
BLANCHE	That won't be necessary. You're a natural gentleman, one of the very few that are left in the world ...

One must conclude that he's a great booby, however worthy a man, and the scene verges on black comedy.

His tragic weakness is pusillanimity: lack of courage, lack of commitment, lack of imagination. When Stanley has cruelly blown the whistle on Blanche, Mitch is torn between puritanical censoriousness at her amours and her drinking, and simple-minded lust:

	(*He places his hands on her waist and tries to turn her about.*)
BLANCHE	What do you want?
MITCH	(*fumbling to embrace her*) What I been missing all summer.
BLANCHE	Then marry me, Mitch!
MITCH	I don't think I want to marry you any more.
BLANCHE	No?
MITCH	(*dropping his hands from her waist*) You're not clean enough to bring in the house with my mother.

As cruel as Stanley, without the hideous courage. He, like Stella, will have to live with Blanche's fate for the rest of his life. A big man, with a small soul.

Thus, *A Streetcar Named Desire*. A profoundly moving play; a picture of modern America coming to terms with the legacy of the past. A play that makes the utmost demands upon the actors, requiring complete verisimilitude, verbal sensitivity, emotional power and delicacy, and courage. But then, all good acting needs courage. It's the badge of the fine actor.

9
Acting Opportunities

Repertory theatre is *dead*. In spite of valiant attempts by the greatly distinguished Peter Hall to revive it, his conception of 'rep' bears no resemblance to the eighty or more companies which used to present a fresh play every week all over the country. Sometimes twice nightly. Actors were engaged on a seasonal basis. To learn, rehearse and act two plays simultaneously; one during the day, a different play rehearsed the previous week during the evening. Some actors performed amazing feats of both memory and performance under these arduous circumstances; I remember particularly the enormously talented Vivien Merchant who, week after week, would give exquisite performances of the greatest range and diversity; also the late Gerald Dawtry at Newcastle, an actor of great versatility and confidence. Grander companies in the great cities would enjoy the luxury of rehearsing and playing for *two weeks*.

It was Hell. On a personal note, I learned nothing from it, except from watching some brave and excellent actors at work, and rapidly resolved to become a director and teacher of acting, with the intent to try to do it better than some of the exhausted and drunken old bullies who had taught me nothing.

How many of today's fine actors survived it, I will never know. Yet turn on your television and you'll see at least a dozen excellent performances a night. There are still a number of fine Flagship Companies in the country, in Glasgow (a national-level company), Manchester, Edinburgh, Plymouth, Leicester, Bristol, the Leeds Yorkshire Playhouse, the Sheffield Crucible and several others but most of these companies must cast on an ad hoc basis, offering the actor a play, or two, or bearing them in mind for a future project.

The present-day young actor must find somewhere else to learn and practise his or her trade. The eminent director John Fernald, later a most charismatic principal of RADA, said that British actors were so good because they spent their lives wrestling with appalling plays: drawing room comedies, murder mysteries, with footling plots and a drivelling dialogue.

The same could be said of the Fringe, but with a different emphasis. Ian Rickson, now Director of The Royal Court theatre, after five years as deputy to Roger Daldry (during which time an awful lot of plays must have been submitted for his scrutiny) uttered the minatory words: *there's a lot of crap out there.*

The Fringe

The Fringe originated as the overflow from the Edinburgh Festival, its most esteemed product being ' Beyond the Fringe', which introduced us to four extraordinary talents – Jonathan Miller, Peter Cook, Dudley Moore and Alan Bennett – all of whom have enjoyed immense success. However, this phenomenon of 'take a chance' theatre has reached a high point of absurdity. At recent Edinburgh Festivals there have been something in the range of six hundred 'productions' on view. My last venture there was a relative success: an excellent play, a fine cast. We played to average audiences of twenty-five. Multitudinous disasters are lucky if they can attract an audience of three or four for two or three nights. Nevertheless, half-an-hour before Curtain Up the cast and I were out in the Lawnmarket handing out flyers to potential punters, and making enthusiastic noises. I was much tempted to utter Ken Tynan's immortal words 'Walk in! Walk in! Thirteen Lovely Girls!' The play itself had a cast of three, and was a very witty Black Comedy about gambling and out-of-work actors. On another occasion I directed a fine comedy, written by a friend, at what was an excellent little venue in terms of space and audience potential. I got together a cast of three of some distinction who, between them, had acted for the RSC, the National Theatre and a successful television series. No mention was made of the actors' enjoying a share of any profit made, but they believed in the play. The cast were excellent, audiences (for the Fringe) not too bad. We, the professionals, were treated with insufferable condescension by the 'producers'. I had made it a condition that, at the very least, they should pay actors' fares or petrol money to get to rehearsal and performance. This was indignantly refused on the grounds that the production hadn't made enough money. *There's a lot of crap people out there.*

What then is the Fringe? Very simply, cheap theatre. This does not necessarily mean bad theatre. Trevor Nunn, a few years ago, suggested that the commercial theatre, as we enjoy and understand it, was likely to disappear and to be replaced by an amorphous form of semi-professional/amateur theatre. (I don't use the word amateur in any pejorative sense, there's a lot of very fine theatre produced by unpaid actors, technicians and directors who have acquired their skills by *doing it.*)

Good and awful Fringe
There is a great crowd of talented, hard–working and well-trained actors desperate for the opportunity to exercise their skills, gain experience, meet challenges. There are many gifted writers and directors finding their way. Such talents are usually sniffed out by small theatres with a reputation for knowing ability in writing and acting – and directing when it comes their way – and indeed seek it out and encourage it. I think particularly of the Bush and the King's Head, in London. The Donmar Theatre, the Hampstead Theatre and the Almeida began as Fringe theatres but the quality of their work over many years has elevated them to major theatre status. Fine and adventurous work also appears at the Tristan Bates Theatre, the Old Red Lion, the New End, the Man in the Moon, BAC, the Grace Theatre and the Finborough Arms. Yet all these brave venues exist on a shoe-string along with several others. The King's Head is trembling on the verge of extinction, whilst profligate opera companies pay tens of thousands of pounds for awful pretentious sets and a few international golden larynxes.

London is thick with Fringe theatres, often performing plays that should never see the light of day. Their substance has preponderantly been agitprop, indignantly but incoherently expressed. The exemplars for Progressive Left liberal theatre must be Shaw, Brecht and Wesker. Sexual agitprop has long been a popular staple, but alas is all too infrequently a plea for personal choice in the disposal of one's affection and sexuality – rather occasions for being bored mindless by characters who insist on giving blow-by-blow accounts of the uniqueness of their sufferings, passions and emotions.

Many fine plays emerge along with the oceans of dross. They enjoy a brief moment of acclaim or condemnation, and are heard of no more. Anything of quality with a smell of success about it is likely to end up at the prestige houses, the National, the RSC or the Royal Court. Writers, actors, technicians and directors sweat their guts out to bring good and bad pieces to theatrical life. The rotten old 'rep' plays, predictable and cliché ridden though they were, did at least trudge from theatre to theatre, in repertory or on tour.

Working conditions
I'll conclude this diatribe by saying that most of the actors and the artists who support them are being conned out of a living by most of the Fringe. Handsome rewards come to a few, but a condition has

been reached where the actor lucky enough to get a part is now expected to exercise his or her talent not just for a lousy wage, but for *nothing*. Fringe plays do not make money. They are lucky if they can recover their production costs. Optimists setting up productions often offer as an allurement the well-known scam 'profit share'. Between you and me, BooBoo, there ain't gonna be no profit!

At present every third person from the left seems to have assumed the mantle of 'director'. Many are muddlers through, amiable and sensible, or odious and tyrannous, or just plain crackpots. Possibly one in twenty has the makings of a really useful director. The same might be said of some of the actors, though the present-day actor is usually a well trained pro: it is astonishing how many actors of proven skills and fine track records will present themselves in all humility when a cast is being solicited for a Fringe or small-scale production. I often read *The Stage* and say to myself, 'What the hell is he or she doing in that load of manifest old garbage in that filthy slum?' The only people likely to make any money out of the enterprise are the owners of such slums, especially sordid rooms over pubs where not only do they charge for rent, they make extra money from liquor sales.

So, the Fringe. The esteemed late director Michael Elliot said some years ago that we must stop creating expensive and grandiose theatres for the old-fashioned purpose of propagating a sort of 'super-rep', or merely to act as Receiving Houses for conventional bums-on-seats tours. Hampstead Theatre, a simple timber prefab, and Greenwich Theatre, a cheap conversion, are two examples of the many less grandiose and more economical buildings. Nevertheless, Greenwich is on the verge of closure, for the want of a measly two hundred thousand pounds a year – in the shadow of the profligate, purposeless Millennium Dome, a billion pound extravaganza. Near-starving actors, designers, directors and technicians are allowed to struggle along in penury.

Small-scale theatre

We must all think profoundly about the purpose and policy of small-scale theatre before lobbying for it with great energy. I feel that closure of bucket-shop drama schools and many fatuous university and college 'drama departments' would be helpful. My vast experience of talking with postgraduate students from these establishments has invariably produced the request: 'But I want to learn *how to act.*'

Small-scale touring

I enjoy the privilege of being on the board of an excellent small-scale touring company. It has a record of fine work under its belt, and during ten years has provided a bare living for the director and a frugal wage for the actors . Fearsome hard work, as we can seldom afford a tour technician and everything has to be carried out by the actors. They get the scenery, costumes and equipment in and out of the venues (very often a school or village hall). They operate the lights and keyboards for sound and music. They strike the set, and put it carefully and exactly in the back of the Transit van. Working largely in the south-east of England we try to get home on most days in order to avoid the expense of digs, though sometimes long engagements are arranged elsewhere (Christmas shows, etc.). A large amount of the work is aimed at schools and young audiences who are enthusiastic and the audience of the future. They must not be played down to, or offered vulgar trendy trash; they want good scripts, good acting and good spectacle.

My directing experience in this métier is with several productions for the excellent Theatre Roundabout, various other ventures and, most particularly, a tour of two striking Noh plays for the Marlowe Theatre at Canterbury, one of which was particularly thrilling and scary. We invariably played to three hundred children at a time and used to count the puddles after each performance. (Not that the purpose of the play was to induce involuntary incontinence.)

Regional theatre touring

There are now a number of modest yet high-quality theatres which must function on a touring basis, particularly in the west of England and rural areas, where there are not enough venues, population or means of transport to sit tight and play for a week or two. Yet there is enthusiasm for good theatre. Scotland shows exemplary resource in getting its skates on and taking theatre to the people. We must bear in mind that we are competing with the sybaritic pleasures of sitting in front of the television with a can of beer and a bag of crisps. Yet I feel with great conviction that touring is one of the most promising forms of theatre of the future. Back to the days of Edmund Kean! He'd act anywhere. We don't need monuments to civic pomp or aldermanic grandeur.

Touring offers the actor the opportunity to develop performance, co-operation with fellow actors and the handling of an audience (persuading them to understand, be moved, be amused and entertained). During the last twenty years, there has been a great volume of condescendingly pretentious and obscure material given an airing, together with production 'styles' which simply haven't worked and which have driven people back to their television.

Dennis Potter said some time ago, 'Television is the people's National Theatre.' I'm all in favour of innovation and adventure: since the end of the nineteenth century we have seen fabulously exciting developments in both matter and manner. Present-day television with its utter believability owes everything to Stanislavsky, Chekhov, Ibsen and Shaw, and to the fascinating writers who have broken moulds since: Brecht, Pinter, Stoppard, even Artaud, and many others. But television is no substitute for the live event. Touring is a great hope for getting the electric excitement of theatre to the people.

Opportunities

Small-scale acting

We must now discuss how the Fringe and small-scale theatre can be of use to the actor. I've held forth at some length about the Fringe, fired by the tattiness in general of its presentation, the paucity of far too much of its material and the gross exploitation of the actor; the actor is in general a trained professional who has sweated blood to acquire the basic skills of the trade and has been exposed to the cut-throat competition of far too many actors competing for far too few jobs. Financial reward is virtually non-existent, so where he would at one time have appeared in rep, the actor must now use the opportunities of the Fringe just to appear in *plays*, to *act*. This is usually on a modest scale which is in many respects like that of television.

Television

Television is most actors' bread and butter, the medium that offers the most money, the most public acknowledgement and, indeed, a lot of creative and artistic satisfaction, since duds do not write for television. I have always marvelled at (and envied) those skilful practitioners who write 'soaps', some of which are admirable as drama, as character drawing and as dialogue. *Coronation Street* springs immediately to mind and one of the oldies, re-aired in the late 1990s, *The Sweeney*. There are plenty of other examples where the viewer, ordinary member of the public or pro, must say, 'By gum, that stirred me/made me laugh, I believed it.' As I said earlier in this book, the public may not know much about acting, but they know a lot about life and people.

The essence of working for the camera is underplaying. Screen acting is contained: the camera can detect falsity and posturing with a cruel and unerring eye, so the acting needs great truthfulness in its proper context. The actor and the camera have the utmost intimacy; the 'projection' and large gestures which are frequently necessary in a theatre building of some size are inappropriate for small Fringe theatres and television (though sometimes necessary in long shot). I remember the very early days of television drama before acting for television was properly understood, when actors applied before the camera the physical dynamism, energy and size that was attractive on stage. Hands and arms, even the tops of heads, kept disappearing from the screen. Most television acting is naturalistic in style, that is, lifelike. This is true even for its sacred monsters, the Alf Garnetts and Bet Lynches – real situations, real people, real behaviour – though most characters are perhaps more ordinary, of less abundant emotion and passion, than the Alfs and the Bets. The very small acting areas played in the Fringe place the actor as close to members of the audience as to the camera. They can *smell* you. When I am involved, I always insist that the actors smell right, if it's possible – exquisite scent or carbolic soap, though I would not insist on sordid or unwashed characters being true to odour. Vladimir and Estragon would be a bit of a turn–off if you caught a realistic niff of 'em!

For the actor playing on the Fringe, television acting is valuable experience in scale, economy, repose and vocal control. All these qualities are needed by the actor working in any medium, but most especially so in very small acting spaces where the physical relationship between characters, often of the greatest dramatic significance, is constrained by sheer lack of *room* .The Gate Theatre, London, is renowned for performing prodigies of skill in presenting plays with many characters on a tiny stage, helped invariably by fine design. Sam Walters in the small pub theatre at the Orange Tree, Richmond, has for many years shown the same sort of adeptness.

T.I.E. and open-air theatre

These are two important sources of experience for the actor. Theatre in Education makes the actor think pretty hard about conveying exact meaning and precise information in such a way that it will not merely be dramatically exciting but remembered. Fortunately this is considered a socially useful purpose for the theatre, though T.I.E. is one of the first educational tools to suffer Local Authority cutbacks. (The actors must be eating too much or enjoying the occasional pint.) There is also a most exciting movement for presenting classic plays, usually Shakespeare, at open-air venues such as the courtyards of Great Houses during the summer. No setting more appropriate can be imagined and let's hope the movement gathers momentum and above all attracts financial resources.

Such presentations should become a substantial part of the professional output. They are usually enthusiastically attended, financially profitable, and often at present the work and effort of dedicated amateurs. It's cheering to think that Great Theatre is not cast in stone and museumed in our two prestige houses.

Perhaps the sort of theatre in the community that Trevor Nunn was speculating about may come to pass. The dramatist and director Anne Jellicoe has for some years been mounting epic productions with Pro/Amateur casts. A brilliant and courageous compromise. A portent of the future?

What next?

If I have taken time in describing the demands made upon the actor in Fringe and small-scale theatre, it is because I think that the actor has more freedom of choice there than in much more lucrative or prestigious places.

Selection of opportunities

An examination of the text is the first 'must'. This must be done reflectively and broadmindedly. In what way could this play work? If I don't understand it, can the director clarify it for me? Can he or she enlighten me about how it should be well acted? What sort of a part am I being offered? There is no point in playing a small dreary part for two Wolverhampton bus tickets. Does it contain something for me to get my teeth into? (However compact the part.) How do I get on with the director? Could I work with him? It needn't be love at first sight but one may think, yes, she talked a lot of sense, was considerate and enthusiastic, and seemed *organised*. What actors might I be working with? (Look out for those known to be difficult and to be temperament–throwers.) Where is it going to be staged, for how long and will any wages and expenses paid? How long is the rehearsal period? Tell me a little about the writer! It would be utopian to expect positive answers to all these questions, but piffle directed by an ogre with a load of deadbeats must be very firmly and politely turned down. The diplomatic way of doing this is to say ' I'm not right for it,' rather than 'It's not right for ME.'

Attitude

I've found during a lifetime in the profession that most actors are a very decent lot. Generally empathic and sympathetic, humane, cultured and civilized, despite the ghastly insecurity, vulgar curiosity and endless rejections to which they are subjected. Of course, they are no saints. The sort of theatre I've been talking about in this chapter makes the utmost demands on the actor. These are

- an endless capacity for hard work
- good humour
- iron control of temper
- great patience – it may be someone else's problem
- unflappability
- quick wittedness
- love of your work
- love of your audience
- ability to negotiate – diplomacy and tact

May I suggest that every actor needs another string to his bow? If you can operate a word processor, cook *well*, lay bricks skilfully, do accounts or dig like the Devil, you will survive between jobs. Poverty and debt are debilitating and demoralising, and the world doesn't owe us a living.

10
Teaching Acting and Learning Acting

I want to discuss a number of points about the teaching of acting, based on my experience of working with professional actors, talented students at the major schools of drama, inexperienced amateurs of all ages, and young people. I have concentrated throughout this book on reasonably concrete skills and ways of going about acting, since so much activity in teaching, learning and exploring the actor's art seems to be concentrated on the 'magical' element of acting. This is often great fun, sometimes ridiculously pretentious, sometimes a valuable stimulant to creativity, often a mystifying waste of time. Having had the joy of working with two generations of actors, including many of the finest actors under the age of fifty or so, I've been deeply involved in the two aspects of their hard work and struggles to master the art and craft of acting. These are to develop themselves as human beings, to increase their understanding, knowledge, insight and imagination; and of equal importance, slowly and patiently to learn the skills of voice and speech, body and movement that turn ideas and insights into performance. Remember, the actor without technique and expressive skills is vocally, bodily and emotionally awkward and confused – not an actor, but some-body who merely wishes to act. He's not an 'amateur', an expression too often used pejoratively and now divorced from its proper meaning of an enthusiast who carries out some activity for the delight of doing so; there are many amateur actors of great imagination and skill, who are as exciting and capable in performance as the good professional. Quite simply, the common denominators such actors share are talent and expertise. Both have learned how to act.

Working within Schools

There are several very different areas for the teacher of acting, and he or she should be clear what different priorities apply. Probably the most difficult field is 'drama' as a subject for schoolchildren and youngsters who have not sought it out from their own enthusiasm. Drama is used here for creative expression, as a tool for the development of skills in language, imagination, relating and communicating, and understanding. As such it could be seen as a way of contributing to the acquisition of social skills and the art of expression, and very useful too. It seems, however, that for many years educational philosophy has been woolly and confused about drama. Many teachers have told me of their unease at the widely held attitude that drama is 'playtime', not taken seriously enough, and having no proper targets and aims. That it is too frequently a save-all for pupils of a generally low level of attainment, and that almost no one fails GCSE drama. There seems to be an emphasis on theatre games and improvisation (both of which are essential), but very little follow-up in the business of text-study, using the freedoms and skills acquired to bring the writer's words *into performance*. Text is far too often ignored, and plays are regarded as belonging to the English department, to be examined as literature only. One despairing teacher of drama at a big city comprehensive in northern England said that the only two plays ever used as text were *Billy Liar* and *A Taste of Honey*; both admirable plays, but seriously underestimating the interest and intelligence of many fifteen year olds, who might derive a lot from Tom Stoppard's *Jumpers* or *Troilus and Cressida*. The value of acting a writer's text is that it helps the student to become deeply involved with somebody else's view of people and the world, and introduces him to experiences outside his own to a wider range of humour, situations, beliefs, dilemmas and above all, language and vocabulary. Only one kid in a thousand may have the talent and inclination to think of a future as an actor or performer. The object of drama as a curricular subject is not to create legions of would-be actors, but to stimulate a capacity for imagination, empathy and understanding, to encourage physical and vocal expressiveness, and a love of language and imagery and expressive movement. So at a later stage, these abilities should be used to mount a play, just as art lessons result in drawings, paintings, sculptures and models, and competitive sport leads to a real game. Fully realised and entertaining music is not mere idle doodling with voices or instruments, but something complete, coherent and full of meaning and feeling. Drama in schools must have these ends in mind, and give a sense of achievement to those who've taken part.

The drama teacher in a school must be a man or woman of many abilities, of passionate enthusiasm and infinite patience. The best teacher should understand and be able to practise the core theatrical skills:

1 An ability to teach basic good speech, that is, clear and expressive, if possible by his or her own example. This does not mean that they need be an actor, but some talent for it and plenty of nerve is a help.

2 A similar capacity to explain movement and create physical performance. The relaxation process explained in Chapter 3 begins to make sense to fourteen to fifteen year olds, but younger kids will simply benefit from an atmosphere of relaxation and fun. A knowledge of mime, and the ability to demonstrate either the effects, or in some cases the details, of movement is a help.

3 Basic directorial skill. The ability to block a simple production, elucidate and explain a play, a scene, a moment. A talent for creating cooperation and a sense of excitement and purpose.

A valuable ability when working with the young is a flair for costume and staging, even if it's only using a hamper of old clothes in a classroom. Dressing up is fun, and as discussed in Chapter 5, is a catalyst to building a character, part of the 'magic' and a stimulus to the imagination. If a play is to be properly mounted, it will need to be set, costumed and lit, so the art department should be enlisted and made to feel part of the whole enterprise.

Demonstrating

It's been theatrical fashion for many years that the director or teacher must not 'demonstrate', that is show an actor how to do a move, say a line, or carry out a bit of business, nor simply explain a meaning that an actor has not grasped. This conduct is regarded as a heresy against creativity and spontaneity, and the individual right of the performer to balls it up in his own way. The result has been a woefully large amount of undirected rubbish in all areas from the fringe to theatres of repute, based on the shaky premise that artistic expression is an inherent quality that all human beings possess, and that their individual outpourings are invariably moving, enlightening and valuable. Bad directors spend many hours burnishing the egos of the ambitious, aggressive and untalented, and waste time and energy in circuitous persuasions when a simple example, acted out would be far more effective. A good director wisely gives very little 'this is how' advice to talented and experienced actors, confident in the belief that they will arrive at meanings, solutions and effects that will surprise and delight him. They might discuss finer points: ambiguity of meaning, the precise significance of a position. Olivier, a great and original actor and a master of all the actor's skills, said that if the director Michel St Denis said 'Two feet further downstage, Larry', he was happy to comply, totally confident of the director's sense of the subtleties of space between actors.

So it's OK to demonstrate. Good professional actors accept it, if it's clear and illuminating. The director or teacher should be careful that it makes a technical point or illustrates a meaning, and however good an actor he or she is, don't act the actor off the stage; they're playing it. Young people especially need this kind of exemplary guidance. It's like a carpenter teaching an apprentice to use sharp tools skilfully so that he doesn't damage fingers and wood. The teachers purpose is to show how. 'How do I do it? Well, here's one way, now find your way. Use the skill I've shown you whilst making it your own.' Actors readily accept instruction from an expert, the teacher of a period dance, the mime artist, the fight arranger. They are revealing ways of *doing it*. Too many directors are only concerned with the meaning and import of the work, and assume that if this is understood by the actors it will, as if by nature, grow into a dramatic shape, an acted form. This is wishful thinking and young people need simple advice on the ways and means of performance, and as much information about character and meaning as they can cope with.

What Do We Act?

Drama is not part of the National Curriculum in Great Britain, but a supporting subject to English. This seems typical of the parsimony that prevails throughout this nation towards the arts. We compare very unfavourably with many other European countries in our expenditure on the performance arts, and television both BBC and independent channels, are the only adequately funded producers of drama of all kinds. If this state of affairs is to change it can only come about by people's demand: by their enjoyment of plays, by their heightened awareness of what is good material. Television by its nature is a passive experience, without the sense of occasion that the theatre creates, and however fine the acting and content of its best offerings, a sole diet of television drama can turn us into a nation of couch potatoes.

Teachers of drama in schools are the creators of audiences of the future, and many of them are heroic in their work to arouse interest in theatre and acting for its own sake. I went to see the remarkable Stephen Reddaway at a west London comprehensive school and was delighted by the atmosphere of excitement that his work was creating.

The pupils were involved in the entire process of putting on a play: rehearsing, making costumes, painting scenery, finding and making beautiful properties, staging and lighting. Everyone had a responsibility which they undertook with enthusiasm, and the walls of the drama room were covered with photographs of his many previous productions. Evidence of prodigious input by a superb teacher, who has also been in the profession and so brings to his work a pro's knowledge and skills. It's work you do for love and artistry.

The value of drama to young people is that it engenders a particular way of thinking and experiencing life, by liberating the imagination, encouraging role-playing, fantasy, and what is known in fashionable Californian circles as 'creative visualisation'. This is a quality of mind that persists and affects men and women in every walk of life. A trader who makes a beautiful arrangement of fruit and vegetables on his barrow is demonstrating it, a scientist conceiving a new plastic material, a carpenter creating a chair, a cook making a meal are all imagining and inventing. Children live in a world of imagination and 'let's pretend' until eleven or twelve. Then the material world intervenes and takes over, with its demands for educational achievement, future job-training, and very often, alas, conformity. Young people receive a deluge of information, advertising, and all sorts of other influences from the media – the seduction of clothes, music and goodies of every kind. So it's more important than ever that youngsters develop and keep a powerful imaginative life – a sense of the mysterious, lovely and fearsome.

Beginnings

Very young children, those say under the age of eleven, will respond to improvisation which asks them to investigate their own world. The subjects are multitudinous: school, teachers, bullying, being black or white, parents, home, holidays, rich people, poor people, wants, desirable things. The teacher should select a situation and encourage the children to play it out. It will proceed in fits and starts, as some kids are more articulate than others, and the child with a strong ego will dominate proceedings if allowed to. Children will at this stage largely play themselves, but a firm line should be drawn between playing characters and merely having a discussion. Encourage mimicry; an impro on a television programme might help this. Let them invent or mimic animated cartoon characters, spacemen and science fiction monsters, sportsmen, heroes and villains. The object must always be to get them to express ideas and feelings about what they see and understand. Ask them to do physical things, encouraging movement and action – a good starter for this is to ask them to pretend that they're eating their favourite food, guzzling yummy stuff with their fingers, and forgetting those table manners they've been taught. Then from yummy to yukky, encouraging exuberant reactions. Make sure that they've decided exactly what they're eating, and try to keep it directed toward comedy and fun. Fantasy and clowning are important in that they should explore the opposite ends of the emotional scale, from the funny to the frightening. Always reassure the children that it's *pretence and play*. Be lavish with praise, encouragement, love.

Introducing text

Children from ten to twelve are often very perceptive. They will begin to need to work on material which has a structure. The teacher might find it useful to create short scenes from books they've read, children's stories, plays and children's plays, and always from stories with dialogue: Dickens, of adult novelists, springs to mind because of the dramatic qualities of his characters and action. (See how easily *Oliver Twist* transmuted into *Oliver!*) The teacher will need to edit dramatic episodes into scenes from five to ten minutes long, becoming a jobbing playwright in addition to clown, nursemaid, father or mother figure, comforter, disciplinarian, administrator, planner and child psychiatrist.

Text work must be pursued, progressing to longer and subtler and more challenging material as the kids get older. I remember a group of young teenagers at a summer school giving a splendid account of Orson Welles' version of Herman Melville's *Moby Dick*, a story of abundant action and epic proportions. The story tells of the hard and dangerous life aboard a whaler in the last century, of a sailing ship, with its half-crazy captain, Ahab in pursuit of the great White Whale, his eternal enemy. There was rich cast of strange and mysterious characters, tattooed men with mysterious pasts, men of all nationalities. The young actors mimed all of the action, shivering in howling gales, drenched by the sea, taking the wheel, handling sails and ropes, lowering the whale-boats, clambering down the lines into them, rowing like demons.

The whale was sighted. The big dramatic moment had arrived. Harpoons were prepared, and hurled, striking the great, in this case invisible, beast; it towed them furiously through the sea, turned on them, crushed their boat to matchwood, and hurled them into the sea, leaving them to swim for their lives. Or deaths.

Moby Dick is an almost ideal text, combining action, story and character. I must add that girls played whalemen just as well as the lads. The choice of material is limitless, and it's up to the teacher to make choices and to direct the work toward interesting text. The only constraint on his freedom is the GCSE syllabus which he should embrace with every enthusiasm, since the choices can be wide and stimulating. Older teenagers are capable of a wide range of work from plays and musicals, and the convention of studio and workshop production has made mounting a play easier and less expensive.

Advanced Teaching

This area covers everyone from the mature and skilled amateur actor to the drama school student to the working pro. The only suitable training for this kind of teaching is professional experience and high specialisation, plus a talent for teaching and a passion for acting. Actors of talent and skill can give acting master-classes, centred round performances and plays in their experience, examining the problems, ways and means of playing certain roles and styles. Director-teachers are principally directors with a good working knowledge of skills and technique, and the patience and concern to help the young actor. Voice, speech, movement, mime, dance, clowning, tumbling and weapon training are all particular skills; the practitioner must not only be an expert in his subject, but possess a comprehensive knowledge of the actor's art, so that he can relate his work to others. The object is to help in the training of the *whole* actor, and problems may be interrelated. A failure to focus the voice and sustain tone may have a physical or psychological origin. Teachers must always be ready for the one-to-one tutorial, when the student can raise both his acting problems and personal problems, and be sure of a sympathetic ear and wise advice, with referral to specialist teachers if need be. The actor is a fragile creature and requires understanding friendship in the expansion of his personality, temperament, knowledge and skills. Tutorials are now an important feature at all drama schools and the teacher must learn how to handle them.

Teaching acting is a vast subject and worthy of the many books written about it. The teacher's role is a hard one, needing skill and sympathy and enthusiasm. In the present educational climate it needs to be more focused on dramatic text of every kind; drama is about plays, screenplays and acting and whereas social ease, greater fluency and expressiveness are amongst its products, the greater, more profound qualities it fosters are those of imagination and creativity, which extend into every part of our lives.

11
The Actor's Progress

Many people come into acting for widely differing reasons. Some want to become a professional actor because they can't imagine any other career or way of life, some because they love acting, plays, literature, film and television. Many are attracted to what they imagine to be big easy money (one of the major delusions), the glamorous people, the Bohemian life-style. The fact is that being an actor is a chancy, often desperate way of living. Out of nearly 42,000 members of Equity, the actor's trade union, 5,000 to 6,000 will be working in any given week, with seasonal variations for entertainments like pantomime and summer holiday shows. On the other side of the coin, talented and skilful amateur actors will never be short of opportunities and offers, provided they have access to companies that mount productions. This is with the proviso that they must earn their living some other way, and dedicate a very great deal of their spare time to their art. Yet they will be making a valuable contribution to the cultural and artistic life of the community.

Good acting is a matter of opinion. Audiences of the stage and screen are very subjective about what they like or approve of, and actors, as the portrayers of life past, present and even future are subject to fashion and fancy. Yet a curious unanalysed common sense prevails as to what adds up to good acting and what reflects the spirit of the age, serving the dramatist's observations on human character in his time or all time. This we might attribute to the influence of the best of the critics and commentators and the gumption of audiences. On the one hand they are cruel piranhas, who have bought the actors for the price of a ticket, to do their suffering for them; on the other, they are people who recognise truth and insight when they see it. *Any* audience will be moved by brave, clear, thoughtful, honest acting, and by joyful, even cruel, comedy. The best actresses and actors in the profession survive by their talent allied to great skills. An actor who is merely a commodity of fashion will sooner or later be out of fashion, like the innumerable pop and rock performers who glitter brightly for a short time, and then are heard no more.

Criticism

The actor's goad – many actors say 'I never read the notices'. Whilst an actor must live in *some* degree of illusion about his charisma, charm and talent, he or she shouldn't live in a world cut off from the public. He must know what critics to respect and take note of, and which critics are high-flown fools or sourpusses. A critic will give a notice to the public of the general effect and import of a play or film, and an opinion as to whether it was worth saying, and whether the actors said it well. Yet critical opinion can sometimes prove very contrary to the opinion of the general public: fine sensitive plays and films have flopped, whilst many a shallow stinker has run for years. But the actor must say, if reviewed 'That was his impression and he is the audience's guide and representative'. All criticism can be useful and can be easily dismissed if perverse or trivial (that's the critic's problem). But a criticism from someone like the late Kenneth Tynan was well worth noting. He could capture the essence of a performance in a few elegant sentences, often causing the actor to think 'So *that's* what I did!' What is the director, but a kindly critic and advisor during rehearsals, when the performance is being created? He is standing in for a future audience as a judge of the actor's believability, clarity in story telling, and ability to move to tears or laughter. Criticism of skill, or lack of it, is often of more significance than criticism of meaning. Actors and critics, even members of the audience, may argue about the interpretation of a character, a speech or a scene, and the actor can usually advance the defence that they thought long and deep, did much research, and rehearsed for six weeks, and believe the interpretation presented to be true. People will generally not risk reputations, integrity and money on grossly perverse, whimsical, or off-the wall interpretations, which can be experimented with more cheaply on the fringe or in the actors' workshop.

The actor must always be technically competent. This means being at the least:

1 Audible – loud enough and clear enough.
2 Relaxed and economical in movement, knowing the moves and business of the production.
3 Knowing the text *infallibly*. Inside out, forwards, backwards, and upside down. And have a very good impression of what the people he's playing a scene with have to say and do.
4 In charge of his or her emotions and fears.
5 Energised and alert.
6 Full of purpose: to convey character, situation, and dialogue to the best of his ability.

An actor who fulfils these basic requirements has already delivered half his obligation to the play, the audience and his fellow actors, and puts himself into the realm where he commands deeper and more subtle criticism or informed and serious praise. Good actors relish above all informed praise from their peers. Max Wall, Tommy Cooper and Eric Morecambe, and in the present time, Billy Connolly, Mike McShane, Ruby Wax, Victoria Wood and Rowan Atkinson are invariably spoken of as 'comedians' comedians'. There is no higher praise than to be thought of as 'an actor's actor'.

All criticism is useful to the actor. It is a barometer of his effect, and he must accept it with common sense, a constructive attitude, and a very large pinch of salt. Whilst the actor must not be a panic-stricken slave to adverse criticism, it's a valuable indicator of a number of things:

- I need to improve voice/speech/movement.
- I need to think more clearly about character/timing/narrative.
- I must think about how I'm being seen as an actor. I must expand my range/not play any more of this kind of character/play more comedy/ I'm good at it/I can play weighty serious people and move an audience.

A last word of warning. Friends and loved ones are usually much too kind.

Where Am I?

What do you need to develop? Being an actor is a process of continuous growth, and the actor, like all other creative artists, never stops learning and exploring new forms and subjects. John Gielgud, at the ripe age of eighty-seven appeared in Peter Greenaway's innovatory film of *The Tempest*; our greatest Shakespearian, the Pope of a noble tradition, happily embarked on a new way of presenting the play, himself speaking all the characters.

Let's start with the youthful beginner. You may be any age between fifteen and twenty-five. If you want to act purely for the fun of it, but not take it up as a profession, the only difference between you and the pro is that you have less time to devote to acting, and you don't need to go to drama school. But you should share the same aim – to be a good and growing actor, and play a large number of parts, whether in an area you're good at, or over a wide range of characters. Knock on the doors of the amateur companies, approach the nearest youth theatre organisation, students' theatre club, any group of people who mount plays, however small or underfunded an outfit it may be.

Get involved in any capacity, helping to paint scenery, hunting props, making the tea, helping stage management or playing any part you're offered, large or small. Part of the experience is not only what you do but observing others. What they do, how they go about it, and how and why they succeed and fail. Stick at it. Acting is not a 'now and then' activity.

Along with the excitement, creativeness and companionship of actual experience, start acquiring the skills this book has been talking about. These are:

1 Relaxation, for body, voice and mind.

2 Work on voice and speech. Buy a book on the subject by one of the acknowledged experts. Your voice may be in the process of change, if you're very young. So be happy to have a young voice if you look young. Don't 'put on' a voice. It will change, with work, time and practice.

3 Acquire fluent and accurate speech. Many young people are afraid of being mocked for 'talking posh', and in Great Britain particularly there is a trendy inverted snobbery among the otherwise intelligent middle class that to be well-spoken marks you out as a snob and a class enemy. This is nonsense. Don't however go to the opposite extreme and speak affectedly, or you'll deserve the ridicule you get.

4 Read voraciously, especially plays. See every play you can, including some very imperfect performances by inexpert actors, just to examine what not to do. Watch television and movies selectively. Consider and make an assessment of every performance you see. Try to get the feel of the actor's personality and skill. Compare different performances by the same actor.

5 Listen to music, to develop your sense of 'tune' and rhythm, absorbing a wide range of music from pop to opera to Bach and Beethoven, especially musical theatre.

6 Explore your own musical skills, especially for singing. If you have a good natural voice, get a singing teacher; if you can't afford that, join a choir or group with a musically skilled leader.

7 Find out if you have any talent for dance, mime and movement, allying this to (1) above. Young and not-so-young people go through agonies of embarrassment about awkwardness, gaucherie, clumsiness. Attend every dance and movement workshop going. Don't worry a bit if you're obviously not going to be a Nureyev or Tommy Tune, it will all be useful.

This advice applies even more to the would-be drama student, but should be taken seriously (not solemnly) by the pure amateur. There's no point in doing a thing badly or half-heartedly. The amateur tradition is a great tradition, in writing, football, music, painting and a host of other activities, but acting has too often been done in a facetious and slapdash way, on the assumption that it's a thing anyone can do. They can, but badly.

The Young Professional

Assuming that you've pursued something like the course I've just outlined, there are two ways to prepare yourself for the profession. The first is via a recognised and reputable drama school, where the student acquires a meaningless diploma (in terms of future work) if he or she stays the course, but gets a lot of valuable experience in acting and a solid grounding in the actor's skills. The other way is to attend the drama department at a university or higher-education college and take a degree in drama. This degree is a more marketable product than a diploma, if you want to teach drama, but carries no guarantee of performance skills. Such courses are very short on training in the actor's art, and are largely knowledge and theory orientated. Having done a great deal of work with gifted postgraduate students at three of the country's major drama schools I have heard this gripe aired by most of the students.

Another entrée to the profession is through the amateur world of the great universities, in the case of Great Britain, Oxford and Cambridge. Oxbridge has thrown up some remarkable talents: all the Pythons, the now very distinguished quartet from *Beyond the Fringe*, Mel Smith, Griff Rhys-Jones, many fine classical actors, a delightful clutch of beautiful and talented young women, and a compact powerhouse of celebrated directors. These people have all moved apparently effortlessly straight into the upper stratum of the profession. It should be remembered that they are very few in number, of quite exceptional talent, and to a man and a woman have shown drive and career skills to make the average executive pale with envy. They would be exceptional in any sphere.

Of these principal alternatives, the most satisfactory is the recognised vocational full-time drama school. There are seventeen such schools in the Conference of Drama Schools, a body which exists to validate their courses, to examine the training and the product – the actor – and to ensure the highest standards in all aspects of teaching performance art. Each has its own ethos and differences of emphasis, but they are remarkably similar in teaching the priorities I've outlined in this book. There are also a number of as yet unaccredited schools, all of which are newish organisations, but which offer a training much the same as the CDS schools, and indeed share many of their faculty members and directors. Training courses are mostly for three years, though a number of schools provide post-graduate courses of a year's duration. These are intensively concentrated on performance skills, and students who have by this time acquired trained and disciplined minds usually respond very well.

There can be little doubt that the young actor benefits from training. It's an overcrowded and cut-throat profession and training teaches him more than acting skills. It teaches him or her the language and ways of the business. How to present himself, acknowledge his strengths and shortcomings, how to set about getting work, how to conduct himself as a performer. A medium like television or film has colossal production costs and demands the utmost efficiency from the actor. Which drama school is a matter of personal choice and which school will offer you a place, and whether you can raise funds for a course of training where fees in the UK work out at about £7,500 per year. It's an investment. In spite of the success and prominence of a number of non-trained talented people, the great body of working actors from the stars to the humblest young spear-carrier have enjoyed proper formal training. The same now applies to skilled theatre technicians of every kind: stage managers, prop-makers, sound technicians, board operators, costume designers and makers, scenic artists and designers. Absolute professionalism is the rule for success and survival, and the highly skilled technician has usually accomplished a two-year course at one of the major schools.

Managing a career is a skill in itself. The business is profligate in its waste of talent and good intentions, and every Equity newsletter carries a doleful list of those who have given up the struggle. The young pro should set out at once to acquire the services of a reputable, well-connected and assiduous agent to negotiate money on his behalf, to find out what work is on offer, and duly send him for auditions and interviews. From there on, it's up to the actor.

Auditions and readings

Auditions and readings are part of the working actor's life. Only very celebrated and sought-after actors don't have to go over this regular hurdle. Two general rules spring to mind. Be prepared; be yourself. An actor should have a variety of very well prepared and well thought out audition pieces up his sleeve for general auditions. He should have at least half a dozen, preferably more, with contrast and variety: a serious piece by Shakespeare, if you can do it well, a funny piece by Shakespeare; a modern speech that suits you down to the ground; and a piece that is in contrast to what you look like. It's most refreshing to see a handsome actor or actress pull a rich, ripe character part out of the bag and equally delightful when an ugly or perhaps nondescript actor plays a suave or romantic charmer with great elegance and style. (For this latter trick, the actor must be sure of the musicality and persuasiveness of his/her speech, and show effortless control and aplomb.) Next, you need a speech for a character of your age, like you. Aim to strike a balance between pieces which are largely narrative and description, and those which are more subjective and emotional, and perhaps favour comedy and narrative. Profound and strongly expressed emotion is very hard to create at 10 a.m. on a wet Thursday in a studio in Soho. Above all, choose what you're good at, and what's good material. Avoid the overworked pieces, but don't bother to hunt out audition pieces for rarity value alone; it's probably a rare speech because it's a lousy play. Directors and casting directors will scratch their heads and mutter 'What the Hell was that? Didn't understand a word of it'. Be prepared to be asked to move to music, to sing and to improvise on suggested ideas.

Wear simple clothes that suit you, and in which you can move easily. You may at times cheat slightly in favour of the type of person they're looking for. It's probably counterproductive to audition for *Grease* wearing a three-piece suit and a necktie, or *La Dame aux Camellias* wearing jeans and a T-shirt. The actor Tom Baker, of *Dr Who* fame, hearing that a Hollywood director was interviewing actors for the key role of the sinister and dissipated monk Rasputin in the movie *Nicholas and Alexandra* jumped into a taxi in full costume between shows at the National Theatre, and saw the director at his hotel. Baker was playing a very similar sort of part in an adaptation of Dostoyevsky's *The Idiot*. He not only looked perfect for the part, but no doubt conveyed the impression that he was a very busy actor working in exalted circles. Perhaps only an actor of Baker's presence and personality could get away with it, but it does make the point: look right.

Be natural and behave normally. Save the histrionics for the acting, and not too much of those. A director tends to think 'Can this person act? Are they vaguely/very right for the role?' 'Could I work with them?' Be polite, friendly and relaxed, but modestly so. Directors recoil in horror from actors who leer and ogle or who give the impression that their suicide will follow immediately if they don't get the part.

Sight reading
Sight reading is a most valuable skill. It needs daily practice. The actor who can lift words off the page, sometimes at very short

notice, has improved his chances of getting work. The important medium of radio drama (fifty years ago one of the greatest acting media in Britain) requires that the actor can rehearse and then record – that is, with the smallest amount of rehearsal, consign a fine accurate performance to tape. A major play is often rehearsed and recorded in three to four days, and a week's instalments of a long-running radio series recorded in one day. Yet this is not superficial or shallow acting; the actors are superb practitioners of sight reading and vocal acting, lightning fast to apprehend the meanings and nuances of a text, and freed from all the other concerns of acting such as learning moves, wearing costume and make-up, learning lines, coping with an audience. Yet it needs an especial skill, great vocal subtlety, interest, variety and control, and often produces great acting. Laidman Browne and Gladys Young of the 1940s and 1950s were major actors by virtue of their versatility, vocal authority and capacity as story tellers. Chris Gittins, Walter Gabriel of *The Archers* (not my favourite radio soap), created a character which became folklore over the years. His performance, like Warren Mitchell's Alf Garnett, was great acting.

When asked to read, the actor must have time to read the script and prepare a short strategy, time to make an intelligent guess at the meaning of the text, the import of the character. If you are asked to read straight off the cuff, they're not worth working for and it will be misery. A reading should aim to be an intelligent and witty exploration of the lines of dialogue on the page; look for humour, look for narrative, look for character. If it's comedy, make an intelligent guess about the tempo and particular points of timing, pauses for example. Don't overact, emote or get worked up with a script in your hand; it's wise to underplay passages of strong emotion if they occur, and perhaps to ask a question or two of the director about the character's temperament and motivation.

Good sight reading has never been more important than in this age of the commercial, the voice-over, and the dubbed film. Actors and actresses of great distinction are happy to voice television and radio commercials because it's very good money for minimal work. What the advertiser is paying for is a lifetime of acting experience, and a familiar or admired voice. Many documentary films are narrated, not by experts in their subject matter, but by actors, who give fluency and colour to the spoken material. Great accuracy is called for and a perfect sense of timing when the actor has to 'lip-synch', that is, speak dialogue exactly synchronised to the movements of another actors' lips on the screen.

The Actor's Progress

Every part played, every audition undertaken, is part of the actor's experience. You learn from everything you do in acting, from your mistakes and successes and those of others. All performances must be reflected upon, not overdoing the self-criticism or praise, but examining what you have done calmly. Actors are by their very nature emotional and easily excitable, and it's difficult to be objective about work which is, more than most work, part of your whole being. Evaluations should come when the actor has rested after a first performance, and should in the early stages be simply about matters of pace and timing, moves and business, audibility and clarity. You should be able to consider the basic mechanics of the performance, and the audience reaction, particularly to comedy. Making an audience laugh is a matter of good timing, good interplay and a clear head. This is simply a matter of good housekeeping. Every audience is entitled to your best efforts.

It's the subsequent considerations that are the most fruitful in terms of artistic development. These may come a week later, six months later, or ten years after a performance, and they are all valuable. Many actors will have had the experience of returning to the script of a play or seeing a performance of it, and thinking 'that's how I should have played that scene' or 'I didn't have enough breath for that long speech'. The actor must be aware of change and development in himself. Certain types of part must be discarded in the course of time but as the actor or actress waves a cheerful goodbye to the young characters, there is the alluring prospect on the horizon of all the wonderful parts you're now old enough to play. If the actor marries experience to ever-growing technical skill, depth and subtlety, there is a most rewarding sense of accomplishment; if every new part is approached by throwing away all you've done before, you won't develop.

Being an actor seems to demand tremendous self-sacrifice and discipline. It does. But an actor must be a rounded person, a full member of society, and should enjoy the pleasures and challenges of life as much as anyone else. The magician-priest role is something he assumes in his study, in the rehearsal room, on the stage, on the set. Whilst many actors are strange and interesting people, they should also eat breakfast, push a lawnmower, take part in sport, love others, have children, have hobbies and holidays and mortgages, in fact be fully paid-up members of the human race.

Being an actor is being a craftsman.

Being an actor is *growing*.

Further Reading

Voice and Speech
Voice and the Actor Cicely Berry (Virgin Books)
Voice and Speech in the Theatre J. Clifford Turner (A & C Black)
The Voice Book Michael McCallion (Faber & Faber)
Clear Speech Malcolm Morrison (A & C Black)
Ideal Voice and Speech Training Ken Parkin (Samuel French)
A Guide to Practical Speech Training Gordon Luck (Barrie & Jenkins)
Voice in Modern Theatre Jacqueline Martin (Routledge)
Voice Production and Speech Greta Colson (Pitman)

Movement and Mime
The Actor and His Body Litz Pisk (Virgin Books)
The Adam Darius Method Adam Darius (Latonia Publishers)
Design for Movement Lynn Oxenford (J. Garnett Miller)
The Alexander Technique Liz Hodkinson (Piatkus Books)
Be A Clown Mark Stolzenburg (Sterling Publishing Co.)
Playing Period Plays Lynn Oxenford (J. Garnett Miller)

Acting and Improvisation
Tyrone Guthrie on Acting Tyrone Guthrie (Studio Vista)
Theatre. The Rediscovery of Style Michel St Denis (Heinemann)
The Actor's Ways and Means Michael Redgrave (Heinemann)
The Craft of Comedy Haggard and Seyler (Nick Hern Books)
An Actor's Handbook Konstantin Stanislavsky (Theatre Arts Books)
The Actor's Eye Carnosky and Saunders (Performing Arts Journal
    Publications)
Respect for Acting Uta Hagen (Macmillan)
Being an Actor Simon Callow (Penguin)
Acting in Restoration Comedy Simon Callow (Applause Theatre Books)
Playing Shakespeare John Barton (Methuen)
The Actor and His Body Cicely Berry (Virgin Books)
So You Want to be an Actor? Adrian Rendle (A & C Black)
An Actor Prepares Konstantin Stanislavsky (Methuen)

Building a Character Konstantin Stanislavsky (Methuen)
Creating a Role Konstantin Stanislavsky (Methuen)
Desperate to Act Anna Scher (Lions Original)
Impro: Improvisation and the Theatre Keith Johnstone (Eyre Methuen)
Improvisation Hodgson and Richards (Methuen)
Theatre Games Clive Barker (Methuen)
The Improvised Play Paul Clements (Methuen)
Improvisation in Drama Frost and Yarrow (Macmillan)
Theatrical Make-up Bert Broe (Pelham Books)
Stage Make-up Richard Blore of Leichner (Samuel French)
The Art of Acting Carlton Collyer (Meriwether)
How to Read a Play Ronald Hayman (Eyre Methuen)
To the Actor Michael Chekov (Harper & Row)
Manners and Movement in Costume Plays Chisman and Raven-Hart
  (Kenyon-Deane)
Beginning Acting Richard Felnagle (Samuel French)
Active Acting Leslie Abbott (Samuel French)
Complete About Acting Peter Barkworth (Methuen)

There are numerous books of audition material for both sexes.
    John Gielgud and Laurence Olivier have both written at length about acting.
    Lastly, for the fun of it,
The Art of Coarse Acting Michael Green (Arrow Books)
I, an Actor Nicholas Craig (Pan)

Some of the older books are classics but may be out of print. Get hold of them if you can.

Index